WHEN STRIVINGS CEASE

REPLACING THE GOSPEL OF SELF-IMPROVEMENT WITH THE GOSPEL OF LIFE-TRANSFORMING GRACE

SIX SESSIONS

STUDY GUIDE + STREAMING VIDEO

RUTH CHOU SIMONS

HarperChristian
Resources

When Strivings Cease Study Guide
© 2021 by Ruth Chou Simons

Requests for information should be addressed to:
HarperChristian Resources, 3900 Sparks Dr. SE, Grand Rapids, Michigan
49546

ISBN 978-0-310-13004-8 (softcover)
ISBN 978-0-310-13005-5 (ebook)

Scripture quotations marked ESV are taken from the ESV® Bible (The
Holy Bible, English Standard Version®). Copyright © 2001 by Crossway, a
publishing ministry of Good News Publishers. Used by permission. All rights
reserved.

Any internet addresses (websites, blogs, etc.) and telephone numbers in this
study guide are offered as a resource. They are not intended in any way
to be or imply an endorsement by HarperChristian Resources, nor does
HarperChristian Resources vouch for the content of these sites and numbers
for the life of this study guide.

HarperChristian Resources titles may be purchased in bulk for church,
business, fundraising, or ministry use. For information, please e-mail
ResourceSpecialist@ChurchSource.com.

First Printing August 2021 / Printed in the United States of America

CONTENTS

A NOTE FROM RUTH

Hey friend,

I hope you've picked up this Bible study because you're tired—tired of striving. Of course, I don't wish for you to be weary, but the truth is: I'm glad you're ready to lay down the exhausting pursuit of self-betterment and find God's remedy for our need for approval and belonging. *When Strivings Cease* is my story of freedom from striving, and this study is a journey through God's Word that will show us why Jesus is better than our very best efforts.

Chances are, like me, you find that in spite of what the latest meme says or what funny video your girlfriend texted you this morning, you still don't feel like you're quite enough. For all that's on your plate, for the kids in your care, for the dreams you have, for the friends you long for, for the ministries you wait on others to start. With so many opportunities and resources available to us, why do we still feel like we're not enough?

Well, perhaps it's because we were never actually meant to measure up by popular opinion, earthly standards, religious ideals, or dream-making aspirations. If you've been fed a steady diet of, "You are enough!", you likely believe it all depends on you. Perhaps you're tempted to believe you just need to try harder, get your act together, make a plan, and execute it with precision. You may feel like you're running on empty . . . because you are.

The "You are enough—just improve yourself" narrative has left so many women like you and me exhausted, worn out, and wondering why we can't figure out how to be satisfied or how to stop striving so anxiously.

The answer we're looking for isn't the latest strategy for self-improvement; it's the enduring gift of amazing grace, through Jesus. Together, we will explore the welcome God meant for us to have by grace, through faith. It is a welcome that replaces striving for approval, striving for self-betterment, and striving to earn love and favor. I am so glad you've picked up this study and are ready to dig into the riches of God's grace, together. I can't wait for you to see just how amazing grace really is!

Because of grace,

HOW TO USE THIS GUIDE

Each week is split into two different sections—one for the video sessions and group discussion, and one for your personal study.

GROUP SESSION

For the group time each week, I invite you to start by reading a quick opening thought together with a short Scripture passage that will be discussed in the video. There's a warm-up question to help you start thinking about what you'll be discussing for the session—you can have a couple of people share their thoughts or let it serve you as more of a rhetorical question.

As you watch the video together, feel free to take notes or just listen. After the video, you'll use the discussion questions to help process what you've heard. You may or may not talk about every question, and that's okay.

Lastly, there's a prayer prompt to help close out your time together.

PERSONAL STUDY

There are five days of personal study for you each session. Four of the days are designed to help you either revisit a biblical truth or remind yourself of the practical application of that truth, and the fifth day is designed to help you slow down and reflect on the session. There will be 1–2 prompts to get you thinking, but this is your space to translate what you're studying into a personal *application*, so feel free to use it in whatever way makes the most sense for you.

Remember, the goal is to let these truths sink in, not to finish a course.

This study is not a formula or a 5–step plan to success with God (it's actually the exact opposite of that kind of thinking!)

This study is intended to draw you closer to the life-changing, life-impacting truths you may have overlooked in the sea of self-reliance.

This study is ultimately not about you; it's about God. Trust me: slow down and take time to consider all that God has done on your behalf, and you, too, will uncover the freedom when strivings cease.

Gather your people, call a friend, and commit to this 6–session journey together. I'm cheering you on and praying for your encouragement!

FAVOR YOU CANNOT EARN

GROUP SESSION

OPENING

Have a volunteer read the opening out loud for the group.

It's that panicked feeling . . . you know, the one that comes to the surface when you see a friend celebrated for an accomplishment, and you think, "Wait, what am *I* doing with *my* life?" Or, it's that sinking feeling when you reach the end of a day filled with little people and you think, "Do I have what it takes to be a mom to these kids?" Or, maybe it's the desperation you feel when faced with the end of a romantic relationship and you wonder, "Wasn't I 'enough' for him?" It's the familiar longing for favor, acceptance, belonging, and the assurance that we've done enough . . . *are* enough. And we all want it.

Friend, if you struggle with these very thoughts, you are not alone. Whether we act like it or not, all of us have known, at some moment in time, the weight of not measuring up, and responded by trying to be *good enough*. Some of us feel trapped in the never-ending hamster wheel of approval-seeking. Our obsession with earning favor influences the way we dress, how we talk, and who we try to impress. And, if we're honest, it influences the way we interact with God.

We were not made to find our worth, favor, or enough-ness in our own efforts. God made a better way! Let's discover His way together.

Focus SCRIPTURE

Open your Bibles and have a volunteer read this session's Scripture out loud for the group. It doesn't matter which translation you have—reading God's Word together is always a good idea!

Ephesians 2:4–10

Warm-Up QUESTION

Take a few moments to think about the question individually before asking for 1–2 volunteers to share their answers with the group.

Share a circumstance or situation in which you've wondered if what you're doing is really enough or a time when you've questioned whether God is pleased with you.

WATCH THE SESSION 1 VIDEO

Feel free to use this space to take notes.

Scriptures referenced in this session:	
Genesis 3	
Romans 5:8	
Ephesians 2:1–10	
Hebrews 4:16	

GROUP
DISCUSSION QUESTIONS

Use the following questions to help process the themes from the video session. You may not get to every question and that's okay!

1. Describe how you have wrestled with approval from either God or another person close to you. In what ways has your wrestling positively or negatively affected how you relate to others and to the Lord?

2. With whom or where have you felt the most "welcome"? What specifically made you feel that way? How has such a feeling impacted your expectations in other relationships and circumstances?

3. For better or worse, briefly explain who or what has most shaped your view of God and His character? Do you believe this influence has been an accurate reflection of God's character or has *it* skewed your understanding of who God is? Discuss the ramifications of this influence.

4. What comes to mind when you hear the words *unmerited favor*? Share your best definition of the word *grace* and compare it to Ruth's definition. How does the idea of never being worthy of receiving a huge gift make you feel?

5. In what specific ways can you fight the current culture of "strive, hustle, earn your place"? Name a few and if you cannot, listen and write down a few ideas to put into practice or try out.

6. Do you find it easier to give or to receive? Why? What is it about giving or receiving that makes you feel good? In what ways do you or don't you translate those feelings to God's feelings for you?

PRAY

Spend some time praying together before dismissing the group.

Take a few moments for group members to share how they think this study will challenge them and then ask one volunteer to close in prayer, asking God, by His Spirit, to open your eyes to who you are, who He is, and how His grace really can change everything.

PREPARE FOR NEXT SESSION

Make time before your next group meeting to work through the personal study on the following pages. Do as much as you can to get the full benefit from the teaching.

FAVOR YOU CANNOT EARN

PERSONAL STUDY

DAY 1 THE REALITY OF SIN

TRUTH

The brokenness you feel is sin,
and sin broke our relationship
with God and His favor.

> This session's study draws from
> themes in chapters 1, 2, 3, 4,
> and 6 of *When Strivings Cease*.

If my goal in this study is to blow you away with the amazing-ness of God's grace (and it is!), I must first remind you how broken we are as sinners apart from grace. We need to take a step back and take a look at a couple of truths:

who the Bible says we are and who the Bible tells us God is. It might feel like review if you've been walking with Jesus for very long *time*, but these truths are foundational to where we're heading, and I want to make sure we're on the same page. (And I promise: these truths are more wonderful than you and I realize day by day!)

If you take even a minute to think about it, the fact that you can't get away from the presence of sin isn't a surprise to you; you know who you really are . . . you know your own thoughts and actions. Truth is, if you're like me, you've spent a lot of time trying to cover up sin on some level, in order to hide the brokenness you feel. We're intimately acquainted with our short-comings, the gaps they create in our lives, and our inability to "fix" our-selves. Do you feel overwhelmed by the brokenness of sin you see and feel at times? I want you to know that you're not alone!

OUR COMMON PLIGHT

It's actually an age-old problem that can be traced back to the first book of the Bible. When Eve doubted God, believed Satan, and ate the forbidden fruit in the garden of Eden, sin entered creation. And every man, woman, and child since then has battled temptation and sin. They have wrestled with the fact that they cannot change who they are at the most basic level. And, even when we want to deny it, or pretend like we're inherently good people who just make bad decisions, we can't get away from what the Bible has to say about it.

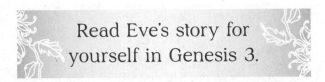

Read Eve's story for yourself in Genesis 3.

It's all over the New Testament, too. In the book of 1 John, the apostle is writing to a group of believers who were wrestling with questions about who they were, in light of some false teaching that had cropped up among them, namely gnosticism.

Gnosticism advocated a belief that maintained that *matter* was inherently evil and *spirit* was good. As a result, gnostics would attribute *some* form of deity to Christ, but they denied His true humanity in order "preserve" Him from evil. Gnostics also claimed to have access to elevated knowledge—basically a higher truth known only to those who were "in" on the deep things. Only the initiated had the mystical knowledge of truth that was higher even than the Scripture. As you can imagine, it was a dangerous belief for followers of Jesus in a lot of ways, one of which was the idea that sin committed in the body had no connection or effect on one's spirit.

This led some people to conclude that sin committed in the physical body didn't matter and that total indulgence in immorality was permissible. Some even took it so far as to deny that sin even existed and disregarded God's law entirely.[1] (Does any of this sound familiar to our current culture?)

All that to say, part of what John addresses in his letter is the reality of the presence of sin. He wants to remind the people of what is true.

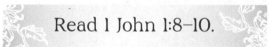

Read 1 John 1:8–10.

● Is it easy or difficult for you to recognize sin in your own life? Why?

● What is your typical response to recognizing sin? Do you rush to cover it up? Quickly confess it to God? Something else?

---

1 "Bible Introductions – 1 John by John MacArthur." n.d. Blue Letter Bible. Accessed July 14, 2021. https://www.blueletterbible.org/Comm/macarthur_john/bible-introductions/1john-intro.cfm.

● What does John say we are doing if we say we have no sin?

There are many passages that tell us about who we are without Christ . . . what our natural default position is. Look up each of the following passages and write down what you learn about human nature from it.

Psalm 14:1–3	
Jeremiah 17:9–10	
Romans 3:23	

Based on these passages, how would you *summarize* what the Bible says about human nature?

Again, if you're being honest with yourself, none of this is news to you, right? And, if asked directly, I doubt if any of us would deny the presence of sin in our lives. But how do our day-to-day actions reflect our awareness of sin? Do we *functionally* believe we're without sin? Are we *practically* making God a liar?

HOPE ON THE HORIZON

If all of this conversation about the reality and presence of sin is weighing on you, stick with me—stunning grace is just around the corner!

Romans 6:23 tells us that the "wages of sin is death." But praise God it doesn't end there—it goes on to tell us that the free gift of God is eternal life!

> *"For the wages of sin is death, but the free gift of God is eternal life in Christ Jesus our Lord."*
>
> **— Romans 6:23 —**

We are sinners with easily deceived hearts, *but* God pursues us with tremendous love and makes a way for us to see sin as the shackle it really is. Jesus is the only one who can rescue us from sin; apart from Him, our sin remains unforgivable, alienating, and blinding in its deception. Grace is this incomprehensible provision that seems both impossible and everything we could ever ask for all at once. Experiencing the grace of God through Jesus's life, death, and resurrection is an incredible gift—one that we'll spend the next six sessions exploring together.

TRUTH

The brokenness you feel is sin,
and sin broke our relationship
with God and His favor.

GET PRACTICAL

If you've already decided to trust Jesus for salvation and His gift of grace, write a prayer below acknowledging who you are without Him and thanking Him for salvation. You might also take this opportunity to confess any sin that the Spirit of God might bring to mind.

Salvation is God's rescue of sinners—forgiving and bringing us near to Himself—that we might be made holy and whole through the blood of His Son, Jesus Christ, as payment for our sin.

If you haven't yet trusted Jesus and are still learning about what it means to follow Him, I'm so glad you're here! I'd love for you to read a note I wrote for you in the Appendix.

DAY 2 AN OLD TESTAMENT PICTURE OF GRACE

TRUTH
Grace is more extravagant than we know.

Grace is a word that gets thrown around a lot, isn't it? Whether it's a pretty plaque at Hobby Lobby, a song on the radio, or a sermon at your church, it's a word you've heard—probably several times. We even used it in yesterday's study! Today we're going to explore what it really *means* by looking at a picture of it in the Old Testament.

If you're a believer, your brain might jump right to Jesus as a picture of God's grace, and you're absolutely right! As it turns out, there are pictures of grace in the Bible long before Jesus comes to earth, too. Grace is part of the story God has been writing from the very beginning.

OLD TESTAMENT GRACE

Every time we catch a glimpse of grace in the Bible, it's designed to point us to Jesus. This is especially true in the Old Testament.

OLD TESTAMENT	NEW TESTAMENT
Books of the Bible focused on God and his people before Jesus' arrival to earth	Books of the Bible focused on Jesus' birth, life, death, and resurrection, as well as the birth of the early church

One of my favorite Old Testament pictures of grace is the story of a guy named Mephibosheth. Mephibosheth was the son of a man named Jonathan and the grandson of a king named Saul. Jonathan was the best friend of David, who reigned as king of Israel in an important era of Jewish history.

The friendship between David and Jonathan was unique—several times the Bible tells us that Jonathan loved David "as he loved his own soul."

Read more about Jonathan and David's friendship	1 Samuel 18:1–4
	1 Samuel 20-14–17
	2 Samuel 1:23–27

Jonathan died in battle when his son Mephibosheth was just five years old. When Mephibosheth's nurse gets the news about Jonathan, she gathers him up to run away (fearing the next wrath of a new king), but he falls and becomes lame.

We don't know a lot about his story after this point until the book of 2 Samuel picks it back up. Many years have passed, and at this point, David has taken his place as king over Israel. He remembers his friend and one day, asks the question: "Is there still anyone left in the house of Saul, that I may show him kindness for Jonathan's sake?"

Indeed, there is—Mephibosheth.

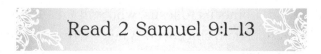

Read 2 Samuel 9:1–13

- How does verse 11 summarize David's attitude toward Mephibosheth?

- How does David show Mephibosheth generosity?

Mephibosheth should have been considered an enemy as the living relative of a previous monarch—that was why his nurse gathered him up so quickly to run when Jonathan died—but David treats him like his own son, inviting him to feast at the king's table for the rest of his life. Do you see grace on display?

PARALLEL STORIES

Consider what the following passages tell us about who we are and what grace does.

- Romans 5:10—Without Jesus we are God's _____.

- Romans 6:23—Because of sin, we deserve _____.

- Romans 8:15–17—Because of grace, God has _____ us into his family.

- Ephesians 1:11—Because of our adoption, we've received an _____ _____.

Do you see the parallels? The way Mephibosheth's story points to our own? We are cast away—far off, removed, and unable to draw near to God until God makes us His children, not because of anything we had to offer—but because of His great and generous love!

Mephibosheth's story points us to Jesus, who will take it even *further* than the account of Mephibosheth can cover. When we receive the grace of God, our favor is fixed for *eternity*.

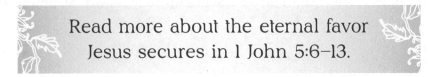

Read more about the eternal favor
Jesus secures in 1 John 5:6–13.

TRUTH

Grace is more extravagant
than we know.

GET PRACTICAL

It might be the most famous verse in the Bible . . . but it's also a wonderful picture of God's generosity, spoken by Jesus Himself.

● Write down John 3:16–17.

● In what ways can the truth in John 3:16–17 change your perspective or encourage you today?

DAY 3 — UNMERITED FAVOR

TRUTH
You can't earn a free gift.

Do you remember the first real paycheck you ever earned? Wasn't it thrilling to hold that piece of paper? (Well, after the disappointment of seeing just how much money was taken out for taxes!) There's a beautiful satisfaction in *earning* something you've worked hard for.

American culture is somewhat famous for a work ethic that promises return on hard work. If you want more money, you can work to make it happen. You can *earn* whatever you set your mind to achieve. While it's an inspiring thought for my fellow entrepreneurs and I, this type of linear relationship *isn't* how grace works.

The simplest definition of *grace* is "generous, unmerited favor." Unmerited means it cannot be earned, but that doesn't mean we don't try, right? It's so unbelievably good that it's hard for us to wrap our minds around it.

We looked at the generosity of grace in the Old Testament yesterday, so today we're adding in the New Testament to help us get a full picture of the scope of grace.

GRACE IN THE NEW TESTAMENT

The Greek word *charis* (which we translate as grace) is used 156 times in the New Testament.

Charis: good will, loving-kindness, favor of the merciful kindness by which God, exerting His holy influence upon souls, turns them to Christ, keeps, strengthens, increases them in Christian faith, knowledge, affection, and kindles them to the exercise of the Christian virtues[2]

Let's start with a quick overview of how the New Testament describes grace. Read the following passages and **write down what you learn about grace from each one**.

John 1:17	
Acts 20:32	
Romans 3:23–24	
Romans 4:7–8	

---

2   "G5485 – Charis – Strong's Greek Lexicon (ESV)." n.d. Blue Letter Bible. Accessed July 14, 2021. https://www.blueletterbible.org/lexicon/g5485/esv/mgnt/0-1/.

Romans 5:1–2	
Romans 5:8	
2 Corinthians 12:9	
Ephesians 1:7	
Ephesians 2:8–9	
2 Thessalonians 2:16–17	

Based on these passages, **summarize** *what* grace is, *where* it comes from, and what it *accomplishes* in your own words.

What grace is:	
Where grace comes from:	
What grace accomplishes:	

A GIFT

In the book of Romans, Paul (we'll talk a lot more about his story in session three) sets out to explain the gospel—that the righteousness of God is available through faith for all who believe.[3] In chapter 5, he talks about how similar to sin coming to all through Adam, the gift of grace has come to all through Jesus.

ADAM	JESUS
Sin enters the world.	Grace comes to the world.

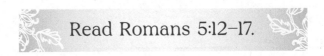

Read Romans 5:12–17.

● How does Paul refer to grace in verse 15?

A quick count reveals that Paul uses this same phrase 5 times in three verses (vv. 15–17). He's really trying to drive it home: **Grace is a *free gift*.**

By nature, "gifts" are intended to be free, right? But I'm sure we've all navigated circumstances where a "free" gift was given, but it held an expectation of reciprocity. It may not cost you anything, but it's not exactly free. Many of us have also found ourselves trying to *earn* something that was intended to be given freely—perhaps the love or approval of a parent?

This is where our personal experiences can taint our view of God and how He works. If you've spent a lot of time trying to earn someone's favor or have been given gifts with an expectation for being "paid back," it's easy to

---

3 "ESV Introductions – Study Resources." n.d. Blue Letter Bible. Accessed July 14, 2021. https://www.blueletterbible.org/study/intros/esv_intros.cfm#at_Romans.

assume that you need to earn God's favor, or that His gifts have strings attached. But that's not how He operates.

Are there specific circumstances that tempt you to think you earn God's grace? Sometimes this lie is so subtle that it's easy to miss. For example, if I have a tough afternoon, I sometimes catch myself thinking, "If I'd read my Bible this morning, this afternoon probably wouldn't be so hard." A friend of mine who was single for longer than many of her closest friends used to wrestle with thinking if she could just "get it together" spiritually, God would send a spouse her way.

While reading my Bible in the morning is a good thing, it doesn't *earn* me God's favor in the afternoon. And my friend wasn't going to *earn* a husband because of something she was or wasn't doing spiritually. Do you see how sneaky believing we have to earn grace is?

- What about you? Where in your life are you tempted to think you need to earn God's grace or favor?

Because our experience and the emotions tied to them aren't always reliable, we have to return to the Word of God over and over to tell us what is true.

- Write Ephesians 2:8–9.

This is what's true! God knew we'd never be able to earn His favor, so He made it a gift we only have to receive.

TRUTH
You can't earn a free gift.

GET PRACTICAL

Rewrite Ephesians 2:8–9 in your own words. (I know this exercise can sometimes feel like an impossible task but putting things into our own words helps solidify them in our hearts and minds. I promise, it's worth the effort! If you get stuck, try reading the verse in several different translations to help you get started.)

DAY  NOTHING TO PROVE IN CHRIST

TRUTH
You have nothing to prove when
your identity is in Christ.

I'm a mom to six young men who regularly find themselves in arm wrestling matches, sprint races, and weightlifting competitions. It's always friendly competition, but these boys are definitely trying to prove something with one another. My version of proving myself is much more subtle (and requires much less physical stamina!). Have you ever relied on your skills, appearance, or achievements to prove yourself? Have you ever tried to establish your worth or detract from your feelings of being "not enough" by being impressive? I know I have.

It's our fallen nature to want to make ourselves look as good as possible—to prove to others, and to God—to secure our own enough-ness with our own abilities. Sin caused us to feel fear and shame, and we've been trying to prove ourselves ever since.

IN THE GARDEN

Let's turn back to Genesis again. We see Eve in the garden of Eden questioning who God has made her to be and whether what He has provided is "enough."

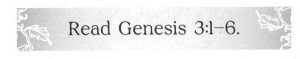

Read Genesis 3:1–6.

- What does the serpent ask Eve in verse 1?

- What lie does the serpent tell in verse 4?

The serpent is exposing an underlying insecurity that Eve has—that the knowledge and sustenance God has given her already isn't enough. That there's more for her to "get."

- How does Eve evaluate the fruit in verse 6? What three things does she notice?

It would taste good, it looked appealing, and it would make her wise. Eating the forbidden fruit seemed to promise her "more."

It's no wonder we battle the same underlying questions about our identity and enough-ness. Like Eve, we look to things that seem to promise us "more" and we throw ourselves into them. We base our identities in what we do, what we don't do, what we own, who we follow, or causes we support . . . even though none of those things will deliver on making us "more."

● What are some things you're tempted to base your identity on?

Even when we *know* the truth—that God's favor is *unmerited*—convincing ourselves that we truly don't have anything to prove is difficult. All it takes is a passing comment, a social media faux pas, conflict with a friend, or too much time in our own heads for our insecurities to surface.

So, what do we do when we find ourselves tossed to and fro? When we **embrace** and **rehearse** the fullness of gospel grace, we're freed to stop the endless pursuit of proving ourselves. We must return to God's Word to rehearse the truth of who we are in Christ and what grace has accomplished on our behalf.

Look at Colossians 3:1–3 with me

"If then you have been raised with Christ, seek the things that are _____ , where Christ is, seated at the right hand of God. Set your _____ on things that are _____ , not on things that are on _____ . For you have died, and your life is hidden with _____ in God."

What two instructions are given here?

1. _____

2. _____

Are the things you're tempted to base your identity on (that you just listed above) things "above" or "things on earth?"

● What's the good news at the end of the Colossians passage?

If you've put your trust in Jesus, your God-given, grace-bestowed identity is secure. You have nothing to prove, friend! In Christ, you are enough and you have enough.

TRUTH
You have nothing to prove when your identity is in Christ.

GET PRACTICAL

Look up each of the following Scripture passages and use what they say about who you are to write an identity statement that begins with, "In Christ, I am . . . ."

WHAT THE WORD OF GOD SAYS	IDENTITY STATEMENT
John 8:36	In Christ, I am . . .
Romans 5:10	In Christ, I am . . .
Galatians 4:4–5	In Christ, I am . . .
Ephesians 1:13	In Christ, I am . . .

WHAT THE WORD OF GOD SAYS	IDENTITY STATEMENT
Ephesians 2:4	In Christ, I am . . .
Philippians 4:19	In Christ, I am . . .
Colossians 1:13-14	In Christ, I am . . .
1 Thessalonians 1:4	In Christ, I am . . .

● Which statement is the most difficult for you to believe or internalize? Why?

● Write a prayer asking God to help you believe what is true and rest securely in your grace-given identity.

DAY  REFLECT

Flip through this session's personal study and write down 1–2 things that stick out to you.

1.

2.

Now, it's time to think about how this applies to your life. Here are a few prompts to get you started. Take some time to reflect and/or journal and pray over what you're learning.

- How have you in the past, or are you now, trying to earn God's favor?

- What examples of God's "generous, unmerited favor" can you see in your life? (Be as specific as possible.)

- Who are you "in Christ," and how does that affect your daily life?

COSTLY, BUT FREE

GROUP SESSION

OPENING

Have a volunteer read the opening out loud for the group.

Last session, we wrestled with the bad news of sin and the incredibly good news of God's grace. My hope is that even for those of us who'd heard these truths before, something stirred in your soul. My prayer is that we now see our great need and God's great provision anew.

Do you sense an awareness of the amazing-ness of grace? An awareness that has perhaps been dulled and dampened by the never-ending message our culture sends through self-help and self-reliance? Can you see how God's grace is so much better than your attempts to earn your way to favor and approval? I sure hope so!

If last session didn't begin to stir your heart and mind to see the hope of the gospel in a new way, I pray this week shakes things up even more. My hope is that this week we'll encounter freedom—a freedom found in discovering all that we've been given through the free gift of grace.

You've heard of the hymn "Amazing Grace," but there's another one you may not know called, "And Can It Be, That I Should Gain?" It was written by Charles Wesley in 1738 and the third verse says this:

> *He left His Father's throne above,*
> *So free, so infinite His grace;*
> *Emptied Himself of all but love,*
> *And bled for Adam's helpless race;*
> *'Tis mercy all, immense and free;*
> *For, O my God, it found out me.*
>
> *Amazing love! how can it be*
> *That Thou, my God, should die for me!*

These words, penned nearly 300 years ago, paint the picture well: "so free, so infinite His grace . . . 'tis mercy all, immense and free." And yet, the cost was that Jesus "emptied Himself of all but love . . . my God, should die for me!" Grace is indeed *free*, but it's not without cost.

Focus SCRIPTURE

Open your Bibles and have a volunteer read this week's Scripture out loud for the group. It doesn't matter which translation you have—reading God's Word together is always a good idea!

Romans 8:32

Warm-Up QUESTION

Take a few moments to think about the question individually before asking for 1–2 volunteers to share their answers with the group.

Have you ever received a gift and then felt like you need to "pay it back" to the gift giver? What made you feel that way?

WATCH THE SESSION 2 VIDEO

Feel free to use this space for notes.

Scriptures
referenced in
this session:

Colossians
2:13–15

Philippians 4:1

Romans 8:31–39

John 6:67–69

GROUP
DISCUSSION QUESTIONS

Use the following questions to help process the themes from the video session. You may not get to every question and that's okay!

1. Do you lean more toward trying to "pay God back" for grace, or living a less than holy life and counting on grace to cover your sin? Why?

2. Do you see your sin as rebellion against God that deserves punishment? In what ways? What has shaped your view of sin?

3. How would you describe the concept of grace to a child?

4. How does accepting "cheap" grace lead to striving? What will prevent us from striving?

5. In what ways do you practically "glorify God and enjoy Him?" How can you help each other do that well?

PRAY

Spend some time praying together before dismissing the group.

Choose one person to pray for your personal study this session, asking that God would help you see the true cost of grace and help you accept it freely for what it truly is.

PREPARE FOR NEXT SESSION

Make time before your next group meeting to work through the personal study on the following pages. Do as much as you can to get the full benefit from the teaching.

COSTLY, BUT FREE

PERSONAL STUDY

DAY 1 REDEMPTION DEFINED

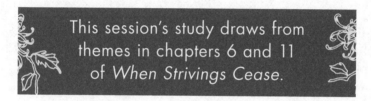

This session's study draws from themes in chapters 6 and 11 of *When Strivings Cease*.

TRUTH
Redemption secures our belonging as beloved.

When I think about how we commonly use the word *redeem* today, one of the first things that comes to mind is a pawn shop. (Stick with me—I promise it will make more sense as we unpack it.) An example might help. Think about it this way: If you've ever sold something to a pawn shop and then decided you wanted it back, you've redeemed your item. There's a sense of "rescuing" something that originally belonged to you and bringing it back into your care again.

We can use this very picture of redemption to help us understand the biblical concept of redemption—God does the rescuing, grants us belonging, and brings us under His care. God Himself pays the price for our welcome, invitation, and belonging as His beloved child. We can confidently say, "I am His and He is mine" (from Song of Solomon 2:16). This assurance is possible because God redeemed us to be His own.

WHAT IS REDEMPTION?

Let's take a look at some passages with a *redeem*, *reclaim*, and *belong* perspective.

Redeem: to liberate by payment of ransom, to buy, to deliver, or by payment of a price to recover from the power of another. It carries with it the idea of freedom and a declaration of rightful belonging.

The first time we see the word *redeem* in the Bible is in Exodus 6, when God promises to redeem Israel.

Read Exodus 6:1–8.

Who is the redeemer?	
Who or what is being reclaimed?	
To whom does the object(s) being claimed belong?	

RUTH

As it turns out, one of the most vivid pictures of redemption in the Old Testament is the story of Ruth. In fact, some people refer to Ruth as the book where redemption is defined. It's a short book and well worth your time to read all four chapters, but for now, let me give you the Cliff Notes version.

In chapters 1 and 2, we learn that Ruth is a young widow who chooses to remain with her mother-in-law, Naomi, after her husband's death. Her mother-in-law is also a widow at this point, so the two of them leave their home to return to Naomi's hometown of Bethlehem. Historically, widows were destitute and often overlooked in society. They were unable to own property, often without a home to live in, and unable to provide for themselves unless a man claimed them into his care.

As a result, Ruth and Naomi arrive in Bethlehem with nothing and no way to provide for themselves. Both by law and by circumstance, their only hope was for a relative to claim them. They needed a kinsman redeemer. The kinsman redeemer was a male relative who, according to the law, had the privilege or responsibility to act on behalf of a relative who was in trouble, danger, or need—he's the one who would deliver, rescue, or redeem the property or person.

> Kinsman redeemers were also expected to take on whatever debt, property, or responsibilities their kin left behind upon their death. They would take it on as their own and in turn redeem the family and property from falling into disgrace.

While Ruth is out gleaning grain in a local field, she has an interaction with a man named Boaz. He finds out who she is and where she came from and grants her favor as she gleans, instructing his servants to leave extra for her to collect. When Naomi learns of Boaz's kindness she's delighted—Boaz is actually a close relative! He is a second-in-line kinsman redeemer for her husband.

Gleaning refers to the custom of allowing the poor to follow reapers in the field and *glean* the fallen spears of grain. It was intentionally set up as part of the law as a provision for the poor (see Leviticus 19:9; 22:2; and Deuteronomy 24:19–21).[4]

Knowing the role that Boaz may be able to play (though he'd have to get permission from the first-in-line kinsman redeemer), Naomi helps Ruth secure Boaz's attention, which brings us to chapter 3.

Read Ruth 3:7–13 and 4:1–10.

Who is the redeemer?	
Who or what is being reclaimed or rescued?	
To whom does the object(s) being claimed belong?	

Let's pause for a minute and think about what we've seen about how redemption works, based on the passages we've read.

---

4 "Gleaning – International Standard Bible Encyclopaedia." n.d. Blue Letter Bible. Accessed July 16, 2021. https://www.blueletterbible.org/search/dictionary/viewtopic .cfm?topic=IT0003828.

- What stands out to you the most?

- What do you think the motivation behind redemption might have been in each scenario? Why was the redeemer so interested in redeeming?

  Exodus:

  Ruth:

- How would you summarize the relationship between redemption and belonging in your own words?

For the person being redeemed, the gift of redemption is belonging as a beloved. Israel was reclaimed as God's beloved, and Ruth and Naomi were rescued to Boaz's care as his beloved. In the same way, you and I are rescued by Jesus—returned to His care and provision instead of under the tyranny of sin.

1 Corinthians 6:19–20 puts it this way:

> ". . . You are not your own, for you were bought with a price . . ."

Tomorrow we'll explore exactly what the price is, but for today, rest in the beauty of what redemption accomplishes!

TRUTH
Redemption secures our
belonging as beloved.

GET PRACTICAL

Based on all you've read in today's study, describe YOUR salvation using
the *redeem*, *reclaim*, and *belong* lens.

Who is the Redeemer?	
Who or what is being reclaimed or rescued?	
To whom does the object(s) being claimed belong?	

● Take a moment to write a prayer thanking God for the redemption
offered in Jesus, and asking Him for help to anchor your heart to Him.

DAY 2 PAID IN FULL

TRUTH
God set the price for our welcome,
and He paid it Himself.

What's the most expensive thing you've ever purchased? A car? A house? A piece of land? A college education? Regardless of what it was, I bet you spent a lot of time saving for it. Or, maybe you're just spending a lot of time paying it off. Either way—saving or paying—likely requires some sort of sacrifice. Not spending your money on something else. Sticking to a budget. Sacrificing time with friends or family to work a job that provides what you need to pay the bills. All things of value take sacrifice to acquire.

That's what makes grace amazing. When we fail to see the great price of our rescue, we miss the wonder of God's grace. The gift that made our belonging, our welcome, our nearness to God possible came at no great cost to us, but meant significant sacrifice to Christ, God's Son. You know the familiar verse, John 3:16:

> "For God so loved the world, that he gave his only Son, that whoever believes in him should not perish but have eternal life."

Out of love, God planned to redeem and rescue His children by sacrificing Jesus—the only one able to live a perfect, sinless life. But why was the price so high? Why did our salvation require death? Rather than requiring perfection from us through self-improvement, God set the price for our return to him by the shelter of Christ's sinless life. We are forgiven because Jesus paid what we owed. This was no afterthought; God sought to reveal His plan of rescue from the beginning.

IT'S ALWAYS BEEN THE PLAN

Believe it or not, the very first book of the Bible points to death and bloodshed being the only acceptable payment for sin.

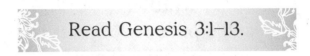

Read Genesis 3:1–13.

Summarize what happens in a few sentences.

God has specific consequences for Adam, Eve, and the serpent as a result of their sin, but read Genesis 3:21.

- What does God do for Adam and Eve after announcing consequences for their sin?

God made clothes for Adam and Eve "from garments of skins . . ." Do you see where I'm going? At least one animal had to die—shed its blood—in order to "cover" Adam and Eve as a result of their sin.

This is just the beginning of how blood and death will continue to play a role in how God relates to his people. Later in the Old Testament, God sets up a sacrificial system for Israel—one that requires the blood of animals to "cover" their sin.

> The sacrificial system required Israelites to offer perfect animals, without blemish, to the priest, who would offer it to God on their behalf. Learn more about the sacrificial system of worship in Leviticus 1–10.

PAID ONCE FOR ALL

It's clear that the *cost* of sin has been death—in fact, the book of Hebrews puts it this way:

> ". . . without the shedding of blood there is no forgiveness of sins." Hebrews 9:22

But it's also clear that the covering provided by the blood of animals was not permanent. The people of God had to offer animal sacrifices over and over again, each time they sinned. This system was in place for a reason, but it wasn't ultimate.

When the Old Testament prophets begin speaking to God's people, they start painting a picture of the day when sin would be defeated once and for all by the coming Messiah.

Messiah: the promised "anointed one" or Christ; the Savior

Prophet: a person chosen to speak for God and to guide the people of Israel

Read Isaiah 53:4–6.

● What does Isaiah tell the people about the coming Messiah?

47

The Messiah is always promised as one who will reconcile the people to God permanently. Jesus proved Himself to be the Messiah by fulfilling every promise made by the prophets—including dying to pay for the sin of every human who has lived, is living, and will live.

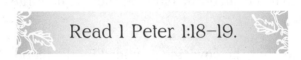

Read 1 Peter 1:18–19.

What does Peter say the believers have been ransomed by?

Jesus lived a perfect life—without sin in any way—which uniquely qualified Him to *pay* for sin in its entirety. We are unable to pay for our sin, reconcile ourselves to a right relationship with God, or fix what's been broken, but Jesus can . . . and did!

THE GOOD NEWS

Followers of Jesus in the New Testament had an entirely different perspective of what His death meant for them because of their familiarity with the sacrificial system. And, as a result, New Testament authors had a lot to say about it.

Read each passage and write down what you learn about Jesus' death as it relates to paying for sin.

2 Corinthians 5:21	
John 3:16–17	
Romans 8:3–4	

Galatians 3:13–14	
1 John 2:1–2	
Hebrews 2:14–17	

Though it is offered freely, grace is made available to us at great cost. Praise God for the sacrifice of Jesus!

GET PRACTICAL

● Based on all we've studied today, describe the tremendous gift of grace in 2–3 sentences.

● Take a moment to write a prayer thanking God for His plan to use Jesus as payment for your sin.

DAY 3 OFFERED FREELY

TRUTH
Grace frees when freely received.

"There's no such thing as a free lunch." I'm sure you've heard this adage before, at least in passing. Apparently, it first appeared as early as the 1930s in response to a common practice of saloons across the United States. In order to entice drinking customers in the afternoon, they would offer a "free lunch." Customers would get a snack or sandwich (high in salt, of course) for "free," but would almost always purchase a drink to help wash it down.[5] These lunches may have been offered freely, but the customers were going to pay the saloon owners one way or the other!

Over time, the phrase has come to express the idea that nothing is totally "free"—somewhere along the way, everything costs someone something. We've spent the last couple of days establishing the price of redemption, the actual *cost* of grace, and the reality that Jesus has paid it. Now, let's look at an astonishing reality: it really is offered *freely*.

POINTING TO JESUS

Grace cost Jesus everything, but He offers it to you and me at no cost, and with no strings attached. It's *actually* free! And, offered freely has been the plan all along. Even in the Old Testament we see beautiful foreshadowing of the *gift* of grace that Jesus will usher into existence.

---

5 Wikipedia Contributors. 2019. "There Ain't No Such Thing as a Free Lunch." Wikipedia. Wikimedia Foundation. May 13, 2019. https://en.wikipedia.org/wiki /There_ain%27t_no_such_thing_as_a_free_lunch.

Isaiah discusses the price of grace, too. See Isaiah 53:4–6.

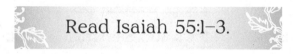

Read Isaiah 55:1–3.

● What is the invitation here?

● Who is the invitation for?

● What are the directions or imperatives in this passage?

Through Isaiah, God invites "he who has no money" to come to the table—to purchase wine and milk for free, and to delight in rich food. John Piper points out that all of the directions/imperatives can be summed up in four words: (1) come, (2) buy, (3) eat, and (4) enjoy.[6] It's that simple! It's quite literally free lunch, but the patron isn't being suckered . . . because the cost has already been covered.

---

6 "The Great Invitation: Come! Drink! Eat! Live!" 1988. *Desiring God*. July 31, 1988. https://www.desiringgod.org/messages/the-great-invitation-come-drink-eat-live.

A PROMISE FULFILLED

This Old Testament picture points us right to Jesus, who fulfills the promise. In John 4, Jesus has an interaction with a Samaritan woman that sounds very familiar in light of Isaiah 55.

> Historically, Jews and Samaritans did not get along and avoided interacting with each other at all costs, so it's particularly interesting that Jesus takes the time to converse with a Samaritan woman.

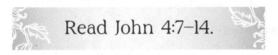

Read John 4:7–14.

● How would you describe the woman's response to Jesus' request for water?

● What type of water does Jesus offer her? How does he describe it?

● What similarities do you see between Jesus' description and the passage in Isaiah?

Jesus *is* the living water and He offers Himself freely to us!

IT'S REALLY FREE

Let's briefly look at a few passages that reiterate the truth that Jesus offers Himself, the grace of God, freely. How does each passage point to the un-merited favor of God being offered *freely*?

Ephesians 2:8–9	
1 Corinthians 2:12	
Matthew 10:5–8	
Titus 3:5	
Romans 5:17	

There are no strings attached, friend. God planned from the beginning to send Jesus to pay the price for sin. Because He pays it *completely,* salvation and the generous, unmerited favor of God are offered to us freely. All we have to do is accept this glorious gift.

Romans 10:9–10 says,

". . . because if you confess with your mouth that Jesus is Lord and believe in your heart that God raised him from the dead, you will be saved. For with the heart one believes and is justified, and with the mouth one confesses and is saved."

It really is that simple. It really is that free. Praise God!

TRUTH
Grace frees when freely received.

GET PRACTICAL

The fact that grace is offered freely is part of what makes it amazing . . . but only if we understand and feel the weight of sin and the cost that has been paid. If we don't identify sin as the problem—not a character flaw or simple mistake—then grace isn't the answer . . . striving is.

Take some time to journal about how understanding that grace is offered freely can help you stop striving.

DAY  ABOVE AND BEYOND

TRUTH
You've been given more than enough.

Imagine walking to your mailbox to grab today's mail and finding an unmarked envelope inside. It sparks your curiosity immediately, so you open it up as you walk back into the house. Inside? The deed to your house with a letter from your mortgage lender declaring that your debt has been paid in full.

What would you do first? Who would you call? How would you celebrate? How many times would you read that letter to make sure you really understood it? How would you feel?

You know what you *wouldn't* do? You wouldn't write a check for your monthly mortgage and mail it in the next day. Or the next month. Or ever again.

Why? Because you're free from that debt! It no longer demands your attention or resources. It's been completely fulfilled, and you no longer answer to the lender.

The same type of exhilarating freedom is ours in Christ because of grace. Our debt of sin no longer demands our striving. It's been completely paid, and we no longer answer to sin.

In both scenarios, it's *abundance* that leads to *freedom*:

- an abundance of wealth (just not yours!) led to freedom from debt, and

- an abundance of grace leads to freedom from sin.

Have you ever thought about the *abundance* of God? He's eternal, self-existent, and the Creator of all things. He has no need and is the beginning of every resource. And He gives *abundant* grace! Part of what's so amazing about grace is that it doesn't just bring our account with God back to a neutral zero. It gives us actual *favor* with God.

Think about it: What we're all striving for is abundance, assurance, favor, and things made right with our Creator, God. We don't just seek to stop striving; we long to be transformed. The gift of grace is *more than* enough for our longing for satisfaction. Grace not only replaces our need for self-improvement, but it makes our life-transformation in fruitfulness possible. We'll get into this transformation more in session four, but first, let's look at the abundant life we access through God's grace.

THE GOOD SHEPHERD

In the gospel of John, we have a record of Jesus telling His followers exactly who He is via seven famous "I am" statements. And one of these statements is directly tied to Jesus' proclamation that He has come to give abundant life to those who believe in Him.

THE 7 "I AM" STATEMENTS	
John 6:35	
John 8:12	
John 10:7	
John 10:11	
John 11:25	
John 14:6	
John 15:1	

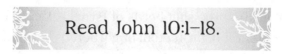

Read John 10:1–18.

- What are the two "I Am" statements in this passage?

We're going to focus on Jesus as the Good Shepherd today, to feel the weight of His promise of an abundant life. We're actually starting in the Old Testament to help us understand the significance of Jesus being the Good Shepherd.

Read Ezekiel 34:1–16

Write down what you learn about the shepherds of Israel and the better shepherd being promised.

SHEPHERDS OF ISRAEL (VV. 1–10)	THE BETTER SHEPHERD (VV. 11–16)

God's indictment against the shepherds of Israel is that they have not done their job! They have not fed, protected, or gathered their flock and the sheep have fallen prey to wild beasts . . . so God tells them that *He* will rescue the sheep (v. 10).

He promises to send a shepherd who will gather the sheep, feed them, strengthen them, and care for them. Do you hear the language of Psalm 23 in there, too?

> *"The Lord is my shepherd; I shall not want.*
> *He makes me lie down in green pastures.*
> *He leads me beside still waters. He restores*
> *my soul. He leads me in the paths of*
> *righteousness for his name's sake."*
> — **Psalm 23:1–3** —

Fast forward to John 10—Jesus is telling the people that He *is* the Good Shepherd! He's claiming to be the promised better shepherd that Ezekiel prophesied about!

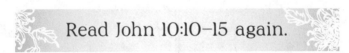

Read John 10:10–15 again.

- What kind of care does Jesus say He will provide for His sheep?

- Why does Jesus say He came? (v. 10)

The Greek word for abundant here is *perissos* and it literally means "over and above, more than is necessary."[7]

Jesus came to earth as the Good Shepherd and though Satan is set on stealing, killing, and destroying, Jesus offers abundant life. More life than is necessary—and only accessible by grace. The generous, unmerited favor we don't deserve and cannot earn, grants us more life and more freedom than we could ever imagine!

THE GIFT OF MORE THAN

Paul talks about this "more than" abundance in his letter to the Romans.

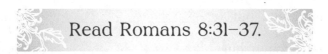

Read Romans 8:31–37.

Look specifically at verse 37:

"No, in all these things we are _____ _____ conquerors through him who loved us."

God doesn't just make us conquerors . . . He makes us *more than* conquerors. It's hard to even wrap your brain around what that means, right? It's just a piece of the abundant life that Jesus' death secured for us. Grace gives us more than we need because God is a generous God.

TRUTH
You've been given more than enough.

---

7 "G4053 – Perissos – Strong's Greek Lexicon (KJV)." n.d. Blue Letter Bible. Accessed July 16, 2021. https://www.blueletterbible.org/lexicon/g4053/kjv/tr/0-1/.

GET PRACTICAL

Look up the following passages to complete the sentences that describe the abundance of grace available to us.

Because of grace, we are:

—More than forgiven, but _____. **Titus 3:4–7**

—More than tolerated, but _____. **Ephesians 2:4–7**

—More than pardoned, but _____. **Romans 8:15**

—More than patched up, but _____. **2 Corinthians 5:17**

—More than found, but _____. **Ephesians 2:6**

—More than enough, but _____. **Colossians 2:9–10**

—More than rescued, but _____. **John 14:1–3**

His abundance is for us, friend!

● Which statement resonates most deeply with you? Why? What changes in your daily life experience knowing these truths?

● Name one lie of the self-striving life you've been believing and claim the truth of God's grace over it.

Spend some in prayer thanking God for His abundance!

DAY 5 REFLECT

Flip through this session's personal study and write down 1–2 things that stick out to you.

1.

2.

Now, it's time to think about how this applies to your life. Here are a few prompts to get you started. Take some time to reflect and/or journal and pray over what you're learning.

Dietrich Bonhoeffer, in his book *The Cost of Discipleship*, wrote about grace like this: ". . . grace is costly because it calls us to follow, and it is grace because it calls us to follow Jesus Christ. It is costly because it costs a man his life, and it is grace because it gives a man the only true life. It is costly because it condemns sin, and grace because it justifies the sinner. Above all, it is costly because it cost God the life of his Son: 'ye were bought at a price,' and what has cost God much cannot be cheap for us. Above all, it is grace because God did not reckon his Son too dear a price to pay for our life, but delivered him up for us. Costly grace is the Incarnation of God."[8]

- What sticks out to you from this quote? How do (or should) these truths affect your day-to-day life?

---

8 Dietrich Bonhoeffer, *The Cost of Discipleship* (London: SCM Press, 2015), n.p.

● How have you personally experienced the "more than" abundance of grace?

● How would you describe the cost of grace to someone else?

RELEASED FROM SHAME

GROUP SESSION

OPENING

Have a volunteer read the opening out loud for the group.

We're talking about a tender topic this session: shame. Whether you're sitting in a room full of other women or alone with your Bible, you know the inescapable feelings of regret, unworthiness, and disbelief that you can be more than the sum of your choices.

Shame is a deep-seated unease that we can't run away from . . . it follows us into relationships, jobs, and every quiet corner of our hearts and minds, constantly whispering I-told-you-so lies about who you are or ever will be.

Regardless of what current culture is trying to sell us, the antidote to avoiding shame is not self-love. It's God's love. The true antidote is understanding that all of redemption is the story of Jesus taking our shame, canceling our debt, and bestowing on us an honor and love we don't deserve. Are you ready to lay down shame for His forgiveness and favor? I promise . . . it's worth it.

Focus SCRIPTURE

Open your Bibles and have a volunteer read this session's Scripture out loud for the group. It doesn't matter which translation you have—reading God's Word together is always a good idea!

Psalm 103:8–13

Warm-Up QUESTION

Take a few moments to think about the question individually before asking for 1–2 volunteers to share their answers with the group.

Is shame something you wrestle with often? What types of circumstances or relationships bring it to the forefront?

WATCH THE SESSION 3 VIDEO

Feel free to use this space for notes.

Scriptures referenced in this session:

Genesis 1–2

Luke 15:11–32

Psalm 103:8–13

GROUP
DISCUSSION QUESTIONS

Use the following questions to help process the themes from the video session. You may not get to every question, and that's okay!

1. Does the relationship between sin and shame, as Ruth explained it, surprise you? Why or why not?

2. When is the first time you recall feeling ashamed? Was it because of your own sin or someone else's sin?

3. How have you experienced the mercy of God running toward you when your shame compelled you to run away from Him?

4. If you had to evaluate your life right now, where do you see yourself in the story of the prodigal son? Why?

5. What are you tempted to base your identity on in this season of life?

PRAY

Spend some time praying together before dismissing the group.

Use Psalm 103 to pray together. Get together in groups of 3 or 4. Begin by having one person read the verse out loud and use it as a springboard for a short personal prayer. You don't have to cover the entire verse in your prayer; you may just find one theme to pray into.

Example:

> Psalm 103:8 "The Lord is merciful and gracious, slow to anger and abounding in steadfast love."

Possible prayer starters:

- Lord, thank you for showing us mercy and grace in . . .

- Your steadfast love is . . .

- Thank you for being slow to anger . . .

Move on to the next person—have them read the next verse and use it as a springboard for personal prayer. Repeat the process until your group has prayed through the entire Psalm.

PREPARE FOR NEXT SESSION

Make time before your next group meeting to work through the personal study on the following pages. Do as much as you can to get the full benefit from the teaching.

RELEASED FROM SHAME

PERSONAL STUDY

DAY 1 THE SHAME OF LEGALISM

TRUTH
Grace is the antidote to shame.

You're not a "good" Christian unless you . . .

If it's easy to fill in the blank for that statement, you've likely had some interaction with the crushing weight of legalism—a set of performative rules that "prove" your spirituality but have nothing to do with the fruit of God's grace in our lives. One of the best definitions I've heard breaks down legalism into two subcategories:

> "First, legalism is treating certain standards as regulations which are kept by your own power in order to gain favor with God. The goal is a better standing with God; the trust is in yourself (not in faith in Christ); and the means is standards of behavior . . . .

"The second definition of legalism is the creation of certain codes of conduct that go beyond the teaching of the Bible and making conformity to these codes critical to being a 'real Christian' or part of the group. The issue here is not so much about favor with God as it is favor with man. The poison of this element of legalism is that it creates an exclusivity based upon standards that are not from God."[9]

What comes to mind for you now? What kind of legalism do you or have you struggled with either now or in the past?

- Treating certain standards as regulations:

- Creating codes of conduct that make you a "good Christian":

I have most certainly fallen prey to legalism at various times of my life. You, too? The message of this book and study has been so important in my life because I've had such a complicated personal battle with striving and performance. In part, due to the fact that Asian culture can itself feel legalistic with high value placed on performance, achievement, and outward standards of honor.

The goal in many Eastern religions is to appease a god through the right set of actions. Good actions lead to (hopefully) a desired response from the impersonal god you worship. Cause and effect. Burn the incense, bring the offering, follow the rules, and you won't be struck down. You may have

---

9 Vroegop, Mark. 2008. "Why Man-Made Rules Don't Work | Sermons." College Park Church. August 31, 2008.https://www.yourchurch.com/sermon/why-man-made-rules-dont-work/.

even been tempted to think of the Judeo-Christian God of the Bible this way, but you'll find through today's study that our grace-giving God is just the opposite—that's what makes grace so amazing! I only found freedom from the "try-harder" method of living when I truly understood God's redeeming grace.

LEGALISM IN THE EARLY CHURCH

Believers in the early church faced a similar battle with legalism and self-righteousness. The scribes and Pharisees loved to create codes of conduct designed to create an "in" crowd for God's people and favor with one another (more on that next week). They made themselves look like they had elite approval from God, but their hearts were not set to worship Him—only to make much of themselves. There was also a type of legalism imposed that taught people there was a standard they could keep that would earn them more favor with God: circumcision.

> Pharisees were a sect of Jewish religious scholars who emphasized outward observance of various rituals and rites as part of worship. Scribes were men intimately familiar with the law because they copied it down word for word. We'll learn more about the Pharisees later in this study.

In Galatians, Paul is making a strong argument for justification (forgiveness, favor and right standing with God) by faith *alone*. Nothing more, nothing less. In chapter 5, he begins with a bold proclamation and then tackles circumcision directly. He's addressing the false teaching that Gentiles (non-Jewish people) must first convert to Judaism and subject themselves to Mosaic law (including circumcision) *before* they could become "real" Christians. Paul wasn't against circumcision in general, but he was absolutely against it being required of Gentiles before being able to follow Jesus.

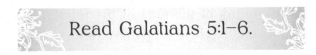

Read Galatians 5:1–6.

● What two directions does Paul give in verse 1?

Look at what he has to say about those who demand justification or right standing through the law.

THE LAW/CIRCUMCISION

● Submitted to a yoke of _____ (v.1)

● Render Christ as no _____ (v. 2)

● _____ to keep the whole law (v. 4)

● _____ from Christ (v. 4)

● Fallen away from _____ (v. 4)

Paul is telling the Galatians that a demand for circumcision as a sign of "true" faith is the opposite of grace. It's at best a misunderstanding of the true nature of grace and, at worst, adding to God's provision as if it were not sufficient on its own. If grace is the generous, unmerited favor of God, demanding anything be added to faith is saying you still have to earn it. It's akin to being invited into an intimate relationship with God, your Father, but then choosing to check off the quiet time boxes on your schedule not to spend time with Him, but to prove that you're doing it right. (Ouch, right?)

Legalism *is* striving and it's bound to bring shame along if the metric for God's happiness with us is dependent on our ability to strive. The gospel is our only hope: Christ has set us free from needing anything but His sacrifice to gain God's favor.

There is, however, a warning attached to the Galatians' freedom. Read Galatians 5:13.

● What is the warning?

Their freedom from the legalistic demands of false teachers was real, but it wasn't an excuse to do whatever they wanted to. How were they to live in freedom, rejecting the legalism knocking on their door, but not go outside of the boundaries provided for their protection *and* to serve one another well while doing it?

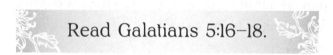

Read Galatians 5:16–18.

● What is Paul's instruction?

The solution is to walk by the Spirit. To literally, "keep in step" with the Spirit. It's the only way we'll be able to use our freedom to serve others instead of ourselves. God's grace gives us access to the power of the Holy Spirit—the power that raised Jesus from the dead! (Romans 8:11) In other words, grace is amazing because we no longer have to strive in our strength alone; we are made right because in Christ, the Spirit goes *with* us, empowers us, and never leaves us.

"If the Spirit of him who raised Jesus from the dead dwells in you, he who raised Christ Jesus from the dead will also give life to your mortal bodies through his Spirit that dwells in you."

Romans 8:11

TRUTH
Grace is the antidote to shame.

GET PRACTICAL

Think back to the types of legalism you have or are wrestling with that you listed at the beginning of today's study.

- How does a legalistic tendency toward religious performance invite shame in your life today?

- How might your everyday life look different if you walk in the freedom Paul describes to the Galatians?

- How does your freedom from legalism and performance translate into service and love to others?

DAY 2 THE SHAME-BEARER

TRUTH
Jesus bears our shame.

This week's study draws from themes in chapters 7 and 14 of *When Strivings Cease.*

Shame can be a powerful motivator, though certainly not a kind one. If we're not aware of what's happening in our souls, feelings of shame can become the primary motivation for how we think, what we do, and what we say. To the casual observer, our actions and words may not be overtly shame-filled . . . but that doesn't mean they aren't. Shame is sneaky and loud all at the same time. Sneaky because it can become so ingrained that we don't even recognize how it's playing out in our lives, and loud because sometimes it's the only voice we can hear clearly as we navigate day-to-day life.

One author put it this way:

> "Because sin is alive in our bodies (Romans 7:23) and because we are beset with weakness (Hebrews 5:2), the kind of shame we often experience is a potent combination of failure and pride. We fail morally (sin), we fail due to our limitations (weakness), and we fail because the creation is subject to futility and doesn't work right (Romans 8:20). We also fail to live up to other people's expectations. And because we are full of sinful pride, we are ashamed of our failures and

weaknesses, and will go to almost any length to hide them from others."[10]

Does that description resonate with you? Take a moment to reflect on your own experience with shame. Think about the following questions in light of your own personal experience, as well as what you've observed in the world and relationships around you.

- What kinds of moral failures/sin cause shame?

- What limitations/weaknesses often lead to shame?

- What brokenness in the world ends in shame?

- What kinds of personal expectations lead to shame?

---

10 "Breaking the Power of Shame." 2016. *Desiring God*. July 15, 2016. https://www.desiring
   god.org/articles/breaking-the-power-of-shame.

The Bible is full of stories of people navigating shame—King David, the woman at the well, the woman who'd been suffering from a bleeding illness, and lepers to name just a few—so it's not surprising that Jesus tackles the topic in a parable, too.

King David	2 Samuel 11
Woman at the well	John 4
Suffering woman	Luke 8:43–48
Lepers	Leviticus 13:45–46 and Luke 5:12–14

THE PRODIGAL SON

The parable of the prodigal son may be familiar (perhaps you've read it a hundred times), but stick with me . . . God's Word is living and transcendent. As many times as we might read it, there are some incredible truths for us to uncover.

Our introduction to the prodigal son is in the middle of a few other parables Jesus is telling the Pharisees (the Jewish religious leaders) as they grumble about with whom he associates.

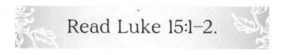

Read Luke 15:1–2.

● What are the Pharisees complaining about?

Because he knows what they're thinking, Jesus starts in on a series of parables . . . and soon we come to the story of the prodigal son.

Prodigal: spending money or resources freely and recklessly; wastefully extravagant

Read Luke 15:11–32 and write down what you learn about each of the characters.

YOUNGER SON	FATHER	OLDER SON

● Where do you see shame playing into this story?

Would you be surprised if I said that all three characters have an interaction with shame in the story? (If you've read *When Strivings Cease*, you probably aren't!) It's true, though! Not only is there a brother who has *acted* shamefully (the younger brother), but there's also a brother trying to *outrun* shame, and a father who is *bearing* shame in order to rescue his son.

YOUNGER SON	OLDER SON	FATHER
Acted shamefully 1. Asked for his _____ before the death of his father (v. 12) 2. Squandered the _____ he was given (vv. 13–14) 3. Lived among _____ which were considered to be the symbol of uncleanness (v. 15) 4. Returned unworthily to his father's house (v. 19)	Trying to outrun shame 1. Responds in _____ over the celebration of his brother's return (v. 28) 2. Self-righteously _____, himself to his brother (vv. 29–30) 3. Believed his obedience should have earned him "more" favor (vv. 29–30)	Bears shame to rescue his son 1. _____ to meet his son, which was unacceptable behavior in Jewish culture (v. 20) 2. By meeting his son while he was far off, he preempted the cultural norms that would have cut his son off from the community and his family for good. (Read a full description of this cultural norm at the end of today's study.)

● Which brother do you most identify with? Why?

Whether you're wrestling with shame over a past action or doing your very best to avoid shame at all costs by "being the best you," God invites you to lay it down. Like the father in this parable, Jesus bears our shame in order to rescue us from sin!

DESPISING THE SHAME

Read Hebrews 12:2 and
then write it here.

The Greek word for "despised" here is *kataphroneō*, and it literally means to "think little or nothing of."[11] Jesus endured death on the cross (the payment required for *our* sin) and "thought nothing of" the shame it meant. What a Savior!

Receiving the gift of grace means that shame has no place. Like the father in the parable, Jesus knows exactly where we've been—every sin, weakness, brokenness, and unmet expectation—and he ran to our defense on the cross. What a Savior!

TRUTH
Jesus bears our shame.

GET PRACTICAL

On a hill far away stood an old rugged cross,
The emblem of suff'ring and shame,
And I love that old cross where the Dearest and Best
For a world of lost sinners was slain.

—"The Old Rugged Cross," George Bennard

11 "G2706 – Kataphroneō – Strong's Greek Lexicon (KJV)." n.d. Blue Letter Bible. Accessed July 14, 2021. https://www.blueletterbible.org/lexicon/g2706/kjv/tr/.

Take some time to meditate on the truths we've studied today:

—God's love is extravagant.

—Jesus bears our shame.

—We have been rescued from sin.

—We are free to approach God confidently because of Jesus.

● Which of these truths resonates with you the most? Why?

● What difference would really believing these truths make for your everyday life?

● Write a prayer of thanksgiving to God for sending Jesus as our shame-bearer.

A NOTE ABOUT CULTURAL NORMS
(An excerpt from *When Strivings Cease*, pp. 98–99)

Kezazah is a ceremony in Jewish cultures that was performed when a Jewish boy lost his inheritance to Gentiles. The ceremony literally meant to be cut off (like "canceled"). Upon his shameful return, the older men of the community would meet the younger man at the city gate and throw a pot down on the ground, signifying the broken relationship and that state of being cut off from his family. A young Jewish male who lost his wealth to a Gentile would not be allowed to return to community. The father was expected to sit, emotionally detached, in his home while the community—the collective—formally deemed the son unworthy.

So why, then, would the father in this parable run to greet his son? While we undoubtedly read into the text an understandable motivation of love and earnest joy in seeing his return, historical context would suggest that the father ran in order to save his son, to redeem his son before the *Kezazah* ceremony could even occur. He preemptively rescued his sinful son by bearing shame himself.

 DAY 3 NO LONGER CONDEMNED

TRUTH
There is no condemnation in Christ.

Do you ever look back on your past and just wish it were different—specifically that you'd made different choices? And by "past" I mean everything from 10 years ago (or longer) to something from last session . . . or even last night. Maybe you feel guilt or shame about something you did or said? Or about something you *didn't* do or say?

One author describes the difference between guilt and shame like this:

> Guilt is usually tied to an event: I did something bad. Shame is tied to a person: I am bad. Guilt is the wound. Shame is the scar. Guilt is isolated to the individual. Shame is contagious.
>
> When you violate God's laws you feel guilt. But that emotion is quickly, nearly simultaneously, joined by shame. Guilt says, "You did something wrong." Shame says, "That's why you need to hide. You're no good. You deserve to live in darkness. Come with me; I'll lead the way."[12]

Unfortunately, more often than not, these emotions linger. They settle into our minds, put down roots, and do their best to destroy hope. Often, these types of emotions are the ones that keep us from "moving on." They keep us bound to the past as we replay the scenarios that surface guilt and the associated shame over and over. As a result, we feel condemned over and over. Grace can help break this cycle, friend!

---

12 DeWitt, Dan. n.d. "The Difference between Guilt and Shame." The Gospel Coalition. https://www.thegospelcoalition.org/article/difference-between-guilt-shame/.

As I mentioned earlier in this session's study, Jesus is no stranger to addressing guilt and shame. Today we'll look more closely at His interactions with one specific woman navigating guilt and shame.

THE WOMAN CAUGHT IN ADULTERY

We've already seen that the Pharisees weren't entirely sure what to do with Jesus . . . they didn't believe him to be the promised Messiah, but they knew he wasn't without power. Over and over, they asked questions to try and "catch" him violating the Old Testament Law.

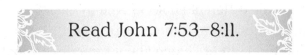

Read John 7:53–8:11.

● Why did the Pharisees bring the woman to Jesus?

● What was the Old Testament punishment for this sin? (See Leviticus 20:10.)

Clearly, the Pharisees weren't as concerned with the Law being broken as they wanted people to believe. If they had been, they would have brought the man who was caught in the act with her. So, what was going on?

The Pharisees were prepared to ridicule Jesus regardless of what His response was—if He confirmed a judgment of stoning, they'd accuse Him of inconsistency since He'd already shown that He was not afraid to associate with sinners. However, if He acquitted her, they'd accuse Him of not upholding or revering Mosaic Law. Either way, they thought they'd be able to trap Him by His response and confirm for themselves that there's no way He could be the Messiah they were looking for.

While the Pharisees plot against Jesus and His ministry, put yourself in this woman's shoes. Caught "in the act" of adultery (v. 6), taken from wherever she was and put on display in the temple while her actions are announced, she stands awaiting a judgment from Jesus. I've always wondered if the women knew who Jesus was. Had she heard of the man who was teaching a new way? Was she hopeful that He would grant her mercy or did she expect death?

If nothing else, the woman must have been feeling guilt—remorse for the event that led to this interaction. Was she also feeling shame? We may not know for sure what she was feeling, but the punishment for adultery definitely carried shame with it. Stoning wasn't about punishing an event; it was about ending the life of a sinful *person*.

And, as we discussed in session one, sin is real. It has real consequences. Our sin "earns" us death. Stoning is what this woman had brought upon herself because of the choices she had made. Yet, Jesus's response is totally counter to the cultural expectations—nor does it fit the mold the Pharisees planned for.

- What is Jesus' response? (vv. 8:7–8)

- How do the Pharisees respond?

Instead of focusing on the woman's actions or character, Jesus asks the Pharisees to look at themselves.

Look at Jesus' final "judgment" in John 8:11:

"And Jesus said, 'Neither do I _____ you; go and from now on _____ no more.'"

The final word here releases the woman from the guilt of her sin and the shame of a stoning death.

NO CONDEMNATION

A few chapters before this exchange, while talking with Nicodemus, another Jewish leader, Jesus has more to say about condemnation.

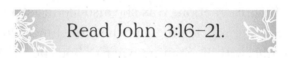

Read John 3:16–21.

● What does Jesus set up as the opposite of condemnation in verse 17?

● In verse 18, what's the difference between being condemned or not?

In His own words, Jesus proclaims His purpose as the opposite of condemning—He came to save! To rescue! He bears our shame by taking all our sin and satisfying God's demand for perfection once and for all!

TRUTH
There is no condemnation in Christ.

GET PRACTICAL

- Is there a specific event, circumstance, or decision from the past (distant or near) that surfaces guilt or shame? Write it down, briefly.

- Do you tend to wrestle more with guilt or shame? (Review the definitions we talked about earlier if necessary.)

- Look up Romans 8:1–2 and write it here.

Now, put your name in the verses and read it out loud.

"There is therefore now no condemnation for _____ because _____ is in Christ Jesus. For the law of the Spirit of life has set _____ free in Christ Jesus from the law of sin and death."

Friend, rejoice in the good news—you have been released from shame!

# DAY 4 FORGIVENESS IN TWO DIRECTIONS

TRUTH
Grace makes forgiveness possible.

Today, I want to help us make the connection between the grace that declares us forgiven and the grace that softens our hearts to forgive those who've wronged us. Grace makes a way for us to be forgiven from sin . . . but grace is also the only way we're able to truly forgive other people. Forgiveness isn't always easy—it's not a button you can just turn on. Our sinful nature wants to keep score, exact payment, and seek revenge. And though we've known the opposite when we receive forgiveness from God Himself, practically living out forgiveness with others (and yourself) as those who are already forgiven can be harder than it seems.

Here are a few questions to ask yourself as we start today's study:

● What do you struggle to forgive in yourself?

● What do you struggle to forgive in others?

● What do you think you need in order to forgive what you answered in the first two questions?

THE UNFORGIVING SERVANT

The apostle Peter often has a reputation for being a little bit rash and sticking his foot in his mouth. While that may indeed be a fair assessment, I can't help but identify with him at times. In Matthew 18:21, he asks Jesus a question we've probably all thought at some point: "Lord, how often will my brother sin against me, and I forgive him? As many as seven times?"

I'm with Peter on this one—wondering how many times I need to forgive someone before I'm "off the hook."

Jesus's answer to the question is stunning.

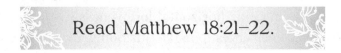

Read Matthew 18:21–22.

● How many times does Jesus say Peter should forgive?

Countless times! One commentary put it this way: "that is, so long as it shall be needed and sought: you are never to come to the point of refusing forgiveness sincerely asked."[13]

---

13 "Commentary on Matthew 18 by Jamieson, Fausset & Brown." n.d. Blue Letter Bible. Accessed July 14, 2021. https://www.blueletterbible.org/Comm/jfb/Mat/Mat_018 .cfm?a=947022.

To further expound on the topic of forgiveness, Jesus tells a parable.

● Read Matthew 18:23–35 and briefly summarize what happens.

● In what ways does this parable relate to your life today?

● How does this parable relate back to Peter's initial question in verse 21?

When we think about forgiveness, we can view it in two directions: vertical and horizontal. And order really matters. Without experiencing vertical forgiveness (from God), horizontal forgiveness (with others) is nearly impossible. The parable serves to make this point: *We* are the servant who has been forgiven much! And because we've experienced the grace of God in the forgiveness from all our sin, we are called to graciously forgive others: seventy times seven.

A QUICK SURVEY OF FORGIVENESS

Let's look at what the Bible has to say about forgiveness. Look up each passage and write down your observations. Take special note of *who* is forgiving, *what* is being forgiven, and what the *conditions* or *circumstances* are for forgiveness. Then, label each passage as a description of vertical or horizontal forgiveness.

PASSAGE	OBSERVATIONS	VERTICAL OR HORIZONTAL?
2 Chronicles 7:14	Who: What: Conditions/circumstances:	
Jeremiah 33:8	Who: What: Conditions/circumstances:	
Matthew 6:14–15	Who: What: Conditions/circumstances:	
Matthew 26:26–29	Who: What: Conditions/circumstances:	
Colossians 3:12–14	Who: What: Conditions/circumstances:	
1 John 1:9	Who: What: Conditions/circumstances:	

● Summarize what you learn about forgiveness from these passages in 2–3 sentences.

FORGIVING EACH OTHER

I don't know about you, but the "one another" commands in Scripture always make me lean in a little bit closer to take note of what's being said. These are the clear words of instruction—and I'm all about clarity! Clarity doesn't mean it's simple or easy, but it does mean God is spelling out what we're called to do.

I don't know if you caught it, but in the survey of passages about forgiveness there was an important "one another" I want to unpack just a bit.

Reread Colossians 3:12–14.

● Before the instruction to forgive, what does Paul tell the Colossians to "put on"?

If we back up even further, to the beginning of chapter 3, we see the big-picture motivation Paul is explaining.

Read Colossians 3:1 and fill in the blanks:

"____ then you have been _____ with _____, seek the things that are above where Christ is, seated at the right hand of God."

IF . . . THEN.

If we've been raised with Christ (i.e., we've received the grace offered to us through His death and resurrection), we can put on what God desires for us. You see, our response of a softened heart is a response to a new state of being, an established condition. Seeking things above doesn't *precede* our changed state by grace; it *follows*.

One pastor unpacked each term like this:[14]

- Compassionate hearts – heartfelt graciousness

- Kindness – an abundance of goodness

- Humility – Christlike dependence on God; submission to Him and to others

- Meekness – display of power under control

- Patience – bearing the exasperating conduct of others

When we rightly recognize who God is and who we are—what we've *received*—we can bear with one another . . . we can *forgive* each other. Listen, if (like me) you struggle to seek and live out these things above (ha, pun intended), you may need to remind yourself of the grace that raised you with Christ. Meaning: we can't forgive or live out the "one anothers" of the gospel if we're not anchored to the very grace that makes a change of heart possible.

- Which of the things from the list above do you struggle with the most? Why?

---

14 Vroegop, Mark. 2008. "Putting on the New | Sermons." College Park Church. September 28, 2008. https://www.yourchurch.com/sermon/putting-on-the-new/.

Grace enables us to do what seems impossible, through the power of the Holy Spirit—praise God!

TRUTH
Grace makes forgiveness possible.

GET PRACTICAL

As we've already established, forgiveness can feel impossible, *but it's not* if it's fueled by a grace-filled understanding of our own forgiveness in Christ. The grace of God that we've experienced is designed to overflow from our lives with just as much humility and generosity as we've been given.

Is there someone in your life whom you're struggling to forgive right now? Perhaps the person who's wronged you has sought forgiveness, but you're still trying him or her in the courtroom of your mind?

Take a minute to reflect:

- What has God forgiven you from? (Get specific!)

- Revisit the definition of grace we discussed on page 23 and write it below.

- Think about a specific way you can show this person grace and write it down.

- If you're still struggling, write an honest prayer asking God to help you give grace and forgive.

DAY  REFLECT

Flip through this session's personal study and write down 1–2 things that stick out to you.

1.

2.

Now, it's time to think about how this applies to your life. Here are a few prompts to get you started. Take some time to reflect and/or journal and pray over what you're learning.

- How has shame affected your life? Where do you wrestle with it most? How has this session's study changed your perspective?

- How does seeing Jesus as the shame-bearer encourage or comfort you?

- How does shame affect your willingness to forgive others? How can you practice forgiveness today?

COMPLETELY CHANGED

GROUP SESSION

OPENING

Have a volunteer read the opening out loud for the group.

The reason why self-help and self-reliance can never lead us to true satisfaction and assurance in Christ is because we were never meant to be simply improved in the first place; we were made to be changed. It's incredibly easy to fall into the trap of thinking of God's grace to simply make ourselves "better." As if it's the formula to living better lives—the secret sauce for being our best selves and achieving every goal we've ever set out to accomplish. It's not just me, right?

If the goal is to become our best, we'll never achieve it. Sin has thoroughly ruined any attempt we might make to achieve perfection. We need a total transformation to address our complete inability to change ourselves. We need a rescuer!

This week, we discover how grace doesn't just pluck us from the pit of self-striving; it transforms us for fruitful living. If you're in Christ, your feelings may need to catch up with the truth you are learning, and that's okay. You are being made new—let's let that change us from the inside out.

Focus SCRIPTURE

Open your Bibles and have a volunteer read this session's Scripture out loud for the group. It doesn't matter which translation you have—reading God's Word together is always a good idea!

2 Corinthians 5:17

Warm-Up QUESTION

Take a few moments to think about the question individually before asking for 1–2 volunteers to share their answers with the group.

What comes to mind when you think about becoming a "new creation" in Christ?

WATCH THE SESSION 4 VIDEO

Feel free to use this space for notes.

Scriptures referenced in this session:	
2 Corinthians 5:17	
2 Corinthians 12:2–10	
John 3:30	

GROUP
DISCUSSION QUESTIONS

Use the following questions to help process the themes from the video session. You may not get to every question, and that's okay!

1. How have you tried to "glue wings on a caterpillar," hoping it will fly? What was the result?

2. We need grace to become a new creation and to continue being made new. How have you experienced both types of grace?

3. What "A+" activities are you tempted to strive for? How did that begin for you?

4. Have you seen a total transformation due to God's grace, either in your own life or someone else's? What did it look like?

5. If you have a desire to change, what keeps you from actually changing? What prevents you from embracing being made new?

6. How is grace different from self-improvement?

PRAY

Spend some time praying together before dismissing the group.

Have one person pray to close your time, asking God to help your group see where they are stuck in a performance mindset, and for individuals to experience freedom in trusting Jesus as the rescuer.

COMPLETELY CHANGED

PERSONAL STUDY

DAY 1 THE PRESSURE TO PERFORM

TRUTH

"Better" is a never-ending
trap that can't save you.

This session's study draws from
themes in chapters 1, 5, 6, 8, and
9 of *When Strivings Cease*.

The pressure to perform can be deceptively convincing. Even if you have a
fairly good grasp of grace, it's easy to fall into the trap of believing that you
just need to *be* better to gain God's actual approval.

In a culture that's constantly telling you to live your best life, speak your truth, tap into your inner strength, and hustle your way to the top, here's the hard truth: Your best efforts, ideas, strategies, and affirmations will *never* be good enough to fix what's really wrong.

Chasing a "better" version of yourself will ultimately lead to despair because, as hard as we try, we'll never be *perfect*. But perfect is the standard required by a holy God. If we don't understand how we can meet God's perfect standard by grace, we will continuously seek to perform our way to reaching those metrics.

> *"For whoever keeps the whole law but fails in one point has become guilty of all of it."*
>
> —— **James 2:10** ——

THE PHARISEES

As we discussed previously, the Pharisees were a sect of Jewish religious scholars who emphasized outward observance of various rituals and rites as part of worship. All throughout the New Testament, we see the Pharisees challenge Jesus and His teachings. In turn, Jesus challenges the Pharisees' thoughts and practices by questioning their heart motivations for worship. When we operate out of a never-ending chase for "better," it's very possible that we're living like Pharisees.

Tim Keller sums it up this way:

> Religious persons obey to get leverage over God, to control him, to put him in a position where they think he owes them. Therefore, despite their moral and religious fastidiousness, they are actually attempting to be their own saviors. Christians, who know they are only saved by grace and can never

control God, obey him out of a desire to love and please and draw closer to the one who saved them.[15]

Ouch. "Attempting to be their own saviors"—have you ever thought about it like that? That your rule-following, be-the-best attitude might actually be an attempt to usurp Jesus as the hero of your story?

In Matthew 15, a group of Pharisees approached Jesus with a question about the "rules." Read Matthew 15:1–2.

● What are the Pharisees concerned about?

● What authority was the rule they were "breaking" under?

The Pharisees were upset about a "tradition of the elders!" It wasn't a matter of the law of Moses—it was a man-made "tradition" that had been set up to hold the same weight as the law. According to one commentary, washing hands at a meal was a practice that the Pharisees placed a "great deal of religion in, supposing that the meat they touched with unwashen hands would be defiling to them." It was strictly observed "as matter of conscience . . . making it a sin against God if they did not do it." In fact, it was so strictly observed that one ancient rabbi equated eating without handwashing as the same as the sin of adultery.[16]

---

15 Keller, Tim. "The Two Prodigal Sons: Reading & Reflection." n.d. Accessed July 14, 2021. https://static1.squarespace.com/static/530e4ef9e4b07ec5e7d89c14/t/57110d6a2b8d dec14befd7b2/1460735338885/The+Two+Prodigal+Sons-+Reading+%26+Reflection +-+by+Tim+Keller.pdf.

16 "Commentary on Matthew 15 by Matthew Henry." n.d. Blue Letter Bible. Accessed July 14, 2021. https://www.blueletterbible.org/Comm/mhc/Mat/Mat_015.cfm?a=944002.

What may have begun as a suggestion to help God's people keep themselves clean and undefiled had taken on far too much weight. Their attempts to be better than even what was required by the Law was backfiring.

● In what ways do you resonate with the Pharisees? What kinds of "extra guardrails" are you tempted to set up for yourself?

Jesus has a very strong response to their question. Read Matthew 15:3–9.

● What commandment does Jesus use to make His point?

● What is His primary indictment against the Pharisees? (v. 7)

In their attempt to add a layer of "protection" to their good works and the law God gave them, the Pharisees have missed the point.

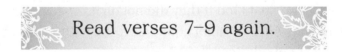

Read verses 7–9 again.

Externally the Pharisees had it all together. They did all the things they were "supposed" to do (and probably lots of things that *weren't* required!), but their actions weren't motivated by a heart of worship. They were replacing God's law—fulfilled God's way—with self-made laws fulfilled in self-satisfying ways. They were trying to be the hero of the story, but they'd never be able to.

It's laughable when we think about it. Just like the law that the Pharisees so "revered" was meant to point them to the Rescuer, *not* themselves, the layers of rules and "should dos" we add to our walk with Jesus are often just about making ourselves look better.

JESUS IS THE ONLY HERO

The author of the book of Hebrews takes on the task of encouraging Jews with the truth that Jesus *is* the Messiah—the Rescuer—the absolute Supreme and Sufficient One.

Read Hebrews 8:6 and fill in the blanks.

"But as it is, Christ has obtained a ministry that is as much _____ _____than the old as the covenant he mediates is _____, since it enacted _____promises."

Much more excellent. Better than the law could ever promise. The hope of every person isn't in being the best, doing the most, or hustling more—it's in Jesus and the generous, unmerited favor of God that we could never earn on our own.

TRUTH
"Better" is a never-ending
trap that can't save you.

GET PRACTICAL

- In what ways are you trying to be your own savior?

- Where are you tempted to see yourself as the hero or the only one who can "fix" what's broken?

- Here's the good news, friend: Jesus *is* the hero! He's the *only* one who is able, and God loved us enough to sacrifice His Son for our rescue. Write a prayer of thanksgiving to Jesus for being the true Savior.

DAY 2 TOTAL TRANSFORMATION

TRUTH
Grace completely transforms us.

Good news won't seem amazing until we know how bad the bad news really is. That's why it's been so necessary for us to really grasp the hopelessness of performing, striving, and earning our way to approval and favor with God.

Yesterday we talked about how, without grace, endless striving for "better" only leads us to despair. When you think about it in these terms, the truth is right in front of us: We need grace to rescue us from *ourselves*.

Today we're going to look at the life of someone we've already mentioned several times: Paul. If ever someone needed rescuing from himself, it's Paul. He was a Pharisee (remember, they didn't get along with Jesus!) who experienced the radical grace of God . . . and it changed him completely.

PAUL'S TRANSFORMATION

PAUL AT A GLANCE

Apostle of Jesus (Romans 1:1; Galatians 1:1)

Started and shepherded churches in Asia Minor and Europe (Romans 1:8–15; 1 Corinthians 1:10–17)

Wrote 13 of the 27 books of the New Testament

One of the most incredible things we know about Paul (who is also called Saul) is the story of his conversion to Christianity—from persecutor of the early church to missionary extraordinaire—it's nothing short of miraculous.

Saul is a Hebrew name interchangeable with the Greek name Paul. Just like many immigrants to English-speaking worlds take an Anglicized name on top of their ethnic name, many Greek-speaking Jews in Paul's day would have a Jewish/Hebrew name and a Hellenistic/Greek name. As he begins his missionary travels, Saul also begins to be known as Paul. (See Acts 13:9.)[17]

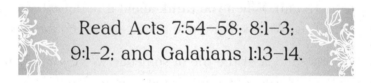

Read Acts 7:54–58; 8:1–3; 9:1–2; and Galatians 1:13–14.

● How would you describe Saul?

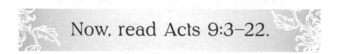

Now, read Acts 9:3–22.

● After his encounter with God, what is Paul like? How would you describe his grace-given identity?

---

17 Lanier, Greg. 2017. "No, 'Saul the Persecutor' Did Not Become 'Paul the Apostle.'" The Gospel Coalition. May 3, 2017. https://www.thegospelcoalition.org/article/no-saul -the-persecutor-did-not-become-paul-the-apostle/.

Total transformation! One of the most beautiful parts of Paul's story is the fact that he never gets over it. He's very aware of God's transforming power in his life because he knows without a doubt that it had nothing to do with him. Left to himself, he never would have changed. He would have continued persecuting Christ-followers and being zealous for the law, without any consideration that Jesus was actually fulfilling the law.

● In what ways is Paul's transformation relevant to your life? How do you relate to his story?

Paul reflects on his transformation in his letter to the Philippians as he reminds them that their only confidence for salvation is God's grace—not anything they can do. In doing so, he compares his old identity with his new one.

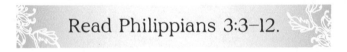

Read Philippians 3:3–12.

● What was Paul's old identity based on? (vv. 5–7)

● What is his new identity based on? (v. 9)

● What do you tend to base your identity on?

● What would change for you if your identity was rooted in the grace of God instead of any attempt at self-improvement?

A NEW BELONGING

Read the following passages and write down how Paul describes himself as he writes to the early church.

Romans 1:1	
1 Corinthians 1:1	
1 Corinthians 3:5	
2 Corinthians 1:1	
Galatians 1:1	
Ephesians 1:1	
Ephesians 3:1	

● What's the overarching theme in these passages? How is Paul primarily identifying himself?

After he encounters the grace of God and is rescued from the penalty of his sin, Paul can't stop talking about *who* he belongs to—who he follows. He's not counting on a long list of accomplishments or the prestige he once sought among Jewish leaders to identify himself—none of the ways he was "better" means anything now. After his conversion, Paul only wants to be known for belonging to Jesus.

● Write Paul's words from Galatians 2:20.

Paul's identity is *so* transformed, that he characterizes his entire life by the life of Christ at work in him! After he meets Jesus on the road to Damascus, the focus of his life is radically altered. His only goal moving forward is to make Christ known. *That* is what it is to live in Christ and Christ in you!

TRUTH
Grace completely transforms us.

GET PRACTICAL

Go back to session one, day four and review what it means to be "in Christ." Choose one statement that you need to be reminded of this week and write down the verse it comes from on an index card. Stick the card somewhere you're sure to see it multiple times this week and work on memorizing it.

DAY  A NEW IDENTITY

TRUTH

You are a new creation.

You're headed to a job interview and you're feeling nervous. You call a friend for a little pep talk before you walk in and their final encouragement is, "Just be yourself!"

Though your friend is well-intentioned, her words make you more frustrated because all you can think is, "But who *am* I?" If you're not confident about who you are and your purpose, that type of encouragement falls flat, doesn't it? Or maybe you know exactly who you are . . . but being your *actual* self feels terrifying because of your view of yourself.

Who we "are" is often summed up in a list of outward-facing characteristics . . . what we wear, whom we call friends, what we do for a job, how we fit into our family units, or our relationship status.

> *"I'm a mom."*
> *"I like decorating with thrift shop finds."*
> *"I'm a teacher."*
> *"I have two siblings.""I'm a teacher."*
> *"I'm single."*

The truth is, whatever facts and words we use to introduce ourselves likely isn't the foundation of who we really are. In Christ we are more than the sum of our likes, dislikes, and even our accomplishments. And, as we'll discover in this session, *who* we are isn't as important as to whom we *belong* and how His grace defines us. If we are to cease striving and walk in the newness of all that grace accomplishes on our behalf, we must rehearse and remember who we really are in Christ.

A NEW CREATION

● Write down 2 Corinthians 5:17.

Now, circle, underline, or highlight the word *new* in the verse.

New: not existing before; made, introduced, or discovered recently or now for the first time.

A NEW creation. The NEW has come.

Just like it did for Paul, grace gives us a new identity—one far better than what we could dream up for ourselves! When we see our identity without the lens of gospel grace, our default posture is striving. When we apply the grace lens, an entirely new identity eclipses the old, because grace changes *everything*.

Notice the verb tense in 2 Corinthians 5:18. If anyone is in Christ, they *are* a new creation. It's a current and ongoing reality, which means you are now free to choose a different way. You're no longer enslaved by sin or by an insatiable desire to be "better."

As followers of Jesus, we know who we *were* before grace and who we now *are* because of grace. And we even know where we're *headed*: being made like Christ through the process of sanctification.

Sanctification: being progressively made more and more like Jesus Christ. (See Romans 8:29.)

In his letter to the Ephesian church, Paul has two goals in mind: first, to remind them what is true about God's grace and their identity in Christ, and second, to instruct them on the implications of God's grace to their daily lives and actions.

Let's look at what he has to say as he reminds the Ephesian believers of what's true.

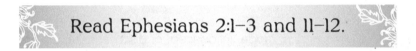

Read Ephesians 2:1–3 and 11–12.

● How does Paul describe the Ephesians before God's grace?

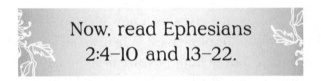

Now, read Ephesians 2:4–10 and 13–22.

● How does Paul describe the Ephesians after God's grace?

● Do any of those descriptions resonate with your own story? Which ones?

● Which descriptions do you find the most joy or comfort in? Why?

A UNIFIED IDENTITY

Another theme throughout the book of Ephesians is beholding the beauty of a church made up of both Jews (God's chosen people from the beginning of redemptive history) and Gentiles alike. Part of what Paul is encouraging the believers to embrace is their identity in Christ above any other identity—even their ethnic identities.

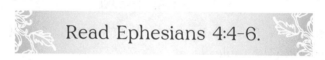

Read Ephesians 4:4-6.

● What is Paul's main point?

The call to unity because of their new identity is a familiar theme for Paul's letters to the early church.

Read Galatians 3:27–29.

● What is the unifying identity Paul describes for the Galatians?

Just like the early church believers, we are called to a *new* identity. We're new creations, and that reality supersedes any other identity we might assume. It unites you with other believers, and it informs every other part of you. Praise God, His grace makes you new!

TRUTH
You are a new creation.

GET PRACTICAL

Review the Scripture from today and, along with your own experiences/memories, complete the table.

Who I was without Christ:	
Who I am in Christ, because of grace:	
What my future holds:	

● Review the memory verse you chose yesterday and write it again here.

DAY 4 A NEW PEACE

TRUTH
Grace allows us to
experience true peace.

Maybe you read today's truth and thought, "I already know I'm at peace with God." And, while you may understand that peace with God has been purchased for you by Jesus' life, death, and resurrection, I want to press in—are you really living out that truth?

Do you often find yourself . . .

- Anxious about the future?

- Wondering if God sees you?

- Worried that God won't answer your prayer because you're not worthy?

- Unsure that God really loves you?

If any of those describe you, you may be missing out on the true peace that grace is offering you. Friend, Jesus has secured peace with God on your behalf! That means you can step into His presence without an ounce of restlessness, insecurity, or anxiety. You belong to Him as a beloved child, and because of Christ, He welcomes you without reservation.

REDEMPTION AND BELONGING

I want to revisit a theme we explored in session 2: redemption. In fact, flip back to session 2, day one. Write down the definition of the word *redeem* that we discussed:

Pay close attention to that last part of the definition: "It carries with it the idea of freedom and a declaration of rightful belonging." In more than one of his letters, Paul reminds believers that because Jesus redeemed them, they belong to God.

Look up the following passages and write down what you observe in each one.

- 1 Corinthians 7:23

- 1 Peter 1:18–19

- Romans 7:4

TRUE PEACE

Being redeemed—rescued and reclaimed—leads us to true peace and security like nothing else can. All of our anxious striving is an attempt to combat the brokenness sin has created. We feel the weight of our sin, and we want to "fix" it, so we do whatever we can to make ourselves better. We use whatever means necessary in an attempt to be "good enough" for God's presence.

If we let it, belonging to God can change the way we approach life. There is peace to be found when we stop striving and simply rest. Below, I've listed a few areas that I've been known to strive in—maybe some of them resonate with you, too.

Read each verse and write down a "peace" application. Because you belong to God, how does the truth of the verse help you experience true peace?

SCRIPTURE	HOW CAN YOU REST BECAUSE YOU BELONG?
For you formed my inward parts; you knitted me together in my mother's womb. I praise you, for I am fearfully and wonderfully made. Wonderful are your works; my soul knows it very well. Psalm 139:13–14	Because I belong to God, I can be at peace with . . .
Love is patient and kind; love does not envy or boast; it is not arrogant or rude. It does not insist on its own way; it is not irritable, or resentful; it does not rejoice at wrongdoing, but rejoices with the truth. Love bears all things, hopes all things, endures all things. 1 Corinthians 13:4–7	Because I belong to God, I can be at peace with . . .
So, whether you eat or drink, or whatever you do, do all to the glory of God. 1 Corinthians 10:31	Because I belong to God, I can be at peace with . . .
Let no one despise you for your youth, but set the believers an example in speech, in conduct, in love, in faith, in purity. 1 Timothy 4:12	Because I belong to God, I can be at peace with . . .

Knowing who you belong to changes everything. From the way you view your body, to the relationships you have, to the way you work, to the ministry you're called to. When you're leaning into the generous, unmerited favor of God, you can experience *true* peace.

TRUTH

Grace allows us to
experience true peace.

GET PRACTICAL

- Historically, is a desire to belong a constant battle for you or not something you've wrestled with much? How does it play out in your life? How does it lead you to striving?

- What can you do to regularly remind yourself that you *belong* to Jesus and let the truth lead you to peace?

DAY 5 REFLECT

Flip through this session's personal study and write down 1–2 things that stick out to you.

1.

2.

Now, it's time to think about how this applies to your life. Here are a few prompts to get you started. Take some time to reflect and/or journal and pray over what you're learning.

- What part of Paul's conversion story resonates with yours? Why?

- What transformation do you see in your life—either compared to when you first decided to follow Jesus or in an ongoing, refining way?

- How does the generous, unmerited favor of God change your belonging and lead you to rest? How can you practically remind yourself of these realities?

- Who else in your life would benefit from understanding these truths?

FREED TO DO GOOD

GROUP SESSION

OPENING

Have a volunteer read the opening out loud for the group.

God restored us to Himself by grace so that we can live, worship, and serve Him as we were created to. Doing good works may not save us, but they are meant *for* us as outworkings of our restored and remade identities in Christ. Right, holy, and good actions were never pitfalls in themselves; it's our attempt to do those things as a means of earning God's favor (and others' too) that is ineffective.

So if we're called to do good, how do we live holy and praiseworthy lives? Does it feel impossible to do good things without striving in your own strength? To be free from the weight of sin and empowered to love and serve without an agenda or ulterior motive? The gospel has good news, friend: Grace makes the impossible possible! Grace frees us to do good.

The generous, unmerited favor of God rescues us from sin *and* empowers us to do what we're called to with a changed heart. We'll never do it on our own, but with grace, we can.

Focus SCRIPTURE

Open your Bibles and have a volunteer read this session's Scripture out loud for the group. It doesn't matter which translation you have—reading God's Word together is always a good idea!

—— Colossians 2:6-7 ——

Warm-Up QUESTION

Take a few moments to think about the question individually before asking for 1–2 volunteers to share their answers with the group.

In Colossians 2:6, what do you think "so walk in him" means?

WATCH THE SESSION 5 VIDEO

Feel free to use this space to take notes.

Scriptures referenced in this session:	
Colossians 2:6–7	
Galatians 5:22–24	
Galatians 5:13	
John 15:4–5	

GROUP
DISCUSSION QUESTIONS

Use the following questions to help process the themes from the video session. You may not get to every question, and that's okay!

1. What burden or weight do you needlessly carry? How do you know it's needless? What's keeping you from laying it down?

2. How does God's grace free us to do good works? How are good works defined in your personal life?

3. What would it practically look like for you to literally "give yourself grace"?

4. How can you anchor yourself to the truth of God's grace to replace striving after good works in your own strength?

5. How can abiding change the way you approach good works? Describe practical ways you can abide in your current daily life.

PRAY

Spend some time praying together before dismissing the group.

Pray together and ask God to show you how to be both unencumbered by sin *and* empowered to do good works by His grace.

PREPARE FOR NEXT SESSION

Make time before your next group meeting to work through the personal study on the following pages. Do as much as you can to get the full benefit from the teaching.

FREED TO DO GOOD

PERSONAL STUDY

DAY WORTHY OF THE CALLING

TRUTH
Because Jesus is worthy, we become worthy by grace.

This session's study draws from themes in chapters 10 and 13 of *When Strivings Cease.*

"She makes the most divine desserts."

"She's the best friend you could ever ask for."

"You could never disappoint me!"

"You're the best mom ever!"

Ever get a title you weren't quite sure you could live up to for the long haul? No matter how kindly the words are spoken, sometimes the expectation they carry feels impossible to bear. At some point, you will make a dessert that doesn't quite hit the mark. Or forget an important date. Or let someone down. Or frustrate your kids. It's bound to happen! Seriously—it's not just me, right?

- What kinds of titles have you been given that made you nervous about your ability to meet expectations?

It's not that big of a deal when your cake falls apart and you "lose" your title, but when the stakes are much higher and you feel ill-equipped to complete the task you've been given, or unworthy to even attempt the task, it's no small thing. It feels overwhelming and even paralyzing.

It's no different in our walk with the Lord. Do you ever worry that you can't do the things you know He's called you to? The roles you've been given to fill? Does it feel overwhelming to move forward? Are you paralyzed with fear and uncertainty?

Here's yet another opportunity for us to rehearse the gospel, friends: We cannot do what we've been called to—any role or task, no matter how significant or insignificant—on our own. Our sin will get in the way every time . . . but God's grace is greater! He takes the most unlikely candidates and uses them for his glory, and the generous, unmerited favor available to us because of Jesus' life, death, and resurrection makes it possible.

Contrary to what the world so often wants to use as encouragement ("You are worthy!"), only the *unmerited* favor of God makes you worthy to do *anything*.

AN UNLIKELY PEOPLE

We've already talked about Israel as God's chosen people . . . but do you know *why* He chose them for Himself? (Hint: It wasn't because they were awesome on their own.)

- What are characteristics in the people you tend to welcome as friends? What are characteristics in people you stay away from and consider *not* worthy of your friendship?

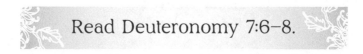

Read Deuteronomy 7:6–8.

- According to this passage of Scripture, what caused God to choose Israel?

The people had nothing to offer God. They weren't a mighty group of warriors God knew he could "win" with. They weren't lovely. They didn't have a great résumé. And God, in His sovereignty, knew their track record wasn't going to improve. They were going to disobey, doubt, and fall into idolatry again and again. And yet—He chose them. *His* faithfulness was the basis for their "worthiness."

Friends, this should stop us in our tracks as we see God's display of love and rescue! He declares loud and clear: We are not loved because we are loveable. We are not worthy because of our astounding good works. It is not on account of our faithfulness that God is faithful. He is the hero!

IT'S ALL GRACE

One of the biggest gifts of grace is that at *every* point in our walk of faith, **God is the one doing the work.** We are *always* on the receiving end—always getting grace.

Look up the following passages and fill in the blank:

Ephesians 1:4	God is the one who _____ you.
2 Timothy 3:16–17	God is the one who _____ you for every good work.
Romans 12:25	God is the one who _____ you.
Jude 1:24–25	God is the one who is able to _____ you from stumbling and present you _____.

We can lay down our ceaseless striving for worthiness because of grace. If you had any doubt, let me lay it to rest: *God is the one who makes you worthy!*

Paul certainly had this truth in mind as he wrote to the church in Thessalonica. Read 2 Thessalonians 1:11–12.

- What does this verse say God will do?

- By whose power will it be accomplished?

- What is the ultimate purpose of God's work?

Paul is reassuring the people by reminding them who their worthiness depends on, whose power will accomplish every "resolve for good and every work of faith," and what the end-goal actually is. Every role you have been called to, and every task God puts before you, depends on grace! His favor frees you to do good—not because you have it all figured out, but because He chose you and he loves you.

TRUTH
Because Jesus is worthy, we
become worthy by grace.

GET PRACTICAL

Take some time to evaluate each question and really take inventory of where your heart is.

- In what areas do you feel unworthy or ill-equipped?

- Be honest with some self-assessment: What things do you say about yourself to others (and to yourself) that reveals your sense of unworthiness?

- What are you basing your worthiness or qualification on? How would you complete this sentence: "I would feel like the girl for the job if only I had more _____."

- If you really understood that God is the one who makes you worthy, what would it look like in your:

  —Relationships

  —Work

  —Family

Take a moment to pray, using 2 Thessalonians 1:11–12 as a template—put your own name into it!

"To this end I pray, that our God may make me, _____, worthy of his calling and may fulfill every resolve for good and every work of faith by his power, so that the name of our Lord Jesus may be glorified in me, _____, and me in him, according to the grace of our God and the Lord Jesus Christ."

DAY 2 FUELED BY GRACE

TRUTH
Good works are only as fruitful as we are deeply rooted in grace.

I hope yesterday's study really convinced you not only that God makes you worthy for what he calls you to, but that his grace is what equips you for the task. But, even when you've settled these truths in your heart and mind, it's easy to fall into a pattern of striving *for* grace, rather than striving *in* grace.

One of the beautiful things about following Jesus is understanding that God **never** demands obedience or fruit apart from a relationship with him. We're never left out in the cold to just "figure it out"—he's with us! Because he's after our hearts more than he's after our actions, he's committed to shaping us . . . in grace.

BACK TO THE BASICS

In Colossians, Paul set up his letter to the church in two big buckets. First, he reminds them who they are in Christ. Then, he talks about how the believers should be acting—the practical outworking of their salvation.

Why did he start with reminding them who they were? They were believers . . . surely, they understood the gospel, right? Paul reminded them because they needed to be realigned to the truth about who they belonged to, who their Father was, and what he had accomplished on their behalf before they were ready to hear instructions on how to live out their faith.

You and I are no different. We need to remember who we are and who God is before we think about how to live out those realities. That's why we started our entire study with those very topics.

Go back to session 1 and review what you learned. Write a 1–2 sentence summary for each topic.

Day One	Who I was without Christ:
Day Four	Who I am in Christ:
Days Two and Three	Who God is and what grace is:

HEAT AND LIGHT

It's like the relationship between heat and light. We need both to survive, just like we need both right *thinking* (light) and right *doing* (heat) One without the other is weak and incomplete. If we overemphasize what we do for God apart from the truth of the gospel, we lack staying power . . . a quick flash of heat, but no light for the long haul. In contrast, if we only ever *think* rightly and never *act*, we may have light, but there is no heat.

> For a more in-depth discussion of this idea of heat and light, see *When Strivings Cease*, chapter 10.

With that in mind, let's look at what Paul has to say to the Colossian church.

● Read Colossians 2:6 and write it below.

Do you see the heat *and* light? Paul calls believers to *action*. They are to "walk in him" because of what they believe. The generous, unmerited favor of God makes it possible to stop striving for ourselves and walk in a way that's motivated by our love for God and his kindness. Knowing *and* doing are fueled by grace.

Let's look at a few examples together. Read each of the following passages and write down the knowledge or truth that's listed and the action that should happen because of it.

SCRIPTURE PASSAGE	KNOWLEDGE/TRUTH	ACTION(S)
Colossians 3:1–3		
Galatians 5:1		
Ephesians 4:17–32		
Philippians 2:13–16		

If you and I can let grace inform our knowledge and, in turn, translate our knowing into doing, it will change everything. Without grace, it's a hopeless balancing act—heat without light or light without heat. But in Christ, because of grace, it's a beautifully choreographed routine.

TRUTH
Good works are only as fruitful as
we are deeply rooted in grace.

GET PRACTICAL

- When you think about your own life, what do you think your biggest struggle is—knowing the truth about who you are in Christ or walking out your faith in light of the truth? Write down a specific example.

- Write a prayer asking God to help you know *and* do in a way that honors Him.

DAY **3** FAITH AND WORKS

TRUTH
True faith works.

The title of this session is "Freed to Do Good," and if you've spent any amount of time thinking about it, it's likely that some questions about the exact nature of faith and works are beginning to surface . . . such as, "If the law points us to grace, does that mean we get to ignore it now? What role does it play in our everyday lives? If grace is really what saves us, do we really need to pay attention to 'good works'?"

If you're wrestling with any of these questions, take heart, friend—you're in the right place and you're definitely not the first person to ask them. It's easy to get your wires crossed and fall either into legalism (like we talked about last session) or licentiousness (disregard for moral goodness), but hopefully you saw yesterday that faith and works really do belong together. They're not just related—they're essential pieces of a whole.

FAITH WITHOUT WORKS IS DEAD

The book of James is full of direct instruction for how believers should live wisely, with unswerving obedience to the Word of God. It's extremely practical and one of the big themes James tackles is this relationship between faith and works.

Read James 2:14–26.

● Summarize James' primary argument—what is his main point?

You can probably sum up the main point of this passage in just five words: Faith without works is dead.

The Greek word for dead here can literally mean deceased or lifeless but it can also mean "inactive as respects to doing right," or, "destitute of force or power, inactive, inoperative."[18] James is telling the believers that their actions matter, because without actions to complete their faith (v. 22), their faith has no power.

Conversely, an active faith that includes good works has *much* power. There are two specific Old Testament examples James points to in order to make his point: Abraham and Rahab.

Read what he says about them and then summarize how their faith and works complemented each other (feel free to read the original stories for more context).

FOR FURTHER STUDY	
Abraham + Isaac	Genesis 22:1–19
Rahab	Joshua 2:1–21

---

18 "G3498 – Nekros – Strong's Greek Lexicon (ESV)." n.d. Blue Letter Bible. Accessed July 14, 2021. https://www.blueletterbible.org/lexicon/g3498/esv/mgnt/0-1/.

	HOW WERE FAITH AND WORKS RELATED?
Abraham	
Rahab	

REPLACING STRIVING WITH ABIDING

If you're like me, the relationship between faith and works isn't necessarily where I get stuck . . . but I do get stuck when it comes to doing the "works" without striving.

Gratefully, over and over I'm reminded that God is after my *heart* more than anything. Just as we touched on earlier, He doesn't demand obedience or the "good-works" fruit of my faith apart from a deep, abiding relationship with Him. The only way we'll ever truly have faith fuel works in a way that isn't striving is if we're *abiding* in Christ.

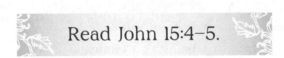

Read John 15:4–5.

● When we abide in Christ, what's the result?

● When we don't abide, what's the result?

If we're all about making our own fruit, we're *striving*. If we're abiding in Christ, good works are the natural outworking of our faith and striving is put to rest. Remember, friend, we already have his favor! Our sin has been covered by the blood of Jesus and his resurrection has secured our worthiness. We have nothing to prove because we brought nothing to the relationship in the first place. The pressure is off when we abide because in Christ; we both *know* the truth and can *do* what's right. Praise God for making a way!

TRUTH
True faith works.

GET PRACTICAL

● Are you abiding or striving today? How? Why?

● How can you move closer to abiding and further from striving? What needs to change?

- Where do you see opportunities for your faith to genuinely fuel good works? (If you get stuck, think about the practical application found in James 2:15–16.)

DAY 4 BOASTING IN OUR WEAKNESS

TRUTH
Weakness isn't to be feared.

Okay, be honest—what's the first thing that comes to mind when you read the title for today's study?

Maybe it was the weakness that you fear? An eye roll accompanied by, "Yeah, right!"? An overwhelming feeling of it just being impossible? A list of insufficiencies you don't ever want called out?

We are intimately acquainted with our weaknesses, aren't we? We do what we can to minimize them, hide them, and beat them . . . but God's grace actually gives us a different lens to see weakness and insufficiency through.

- What if every weakness you experience is an opportunity to see Jesus more clearly?

- What if instead of worrying about, covering up, and feeling shame over the things you don't do well or wrestle with on a regular basis, you could *boast* about them?

Paul talks about this very scenario in his second letter to the Corinthian church.

SUFFERING AND WEAKNESS

In his first letter to the Corinthians, Paul's primary focus is correcting some of their behaviors and encouraging the church to remain unified around the gospel.

> *"I appeal to you, brothers, by the name of our Lord*
> *Jesus Christ, that all of you agree, and that there*
> *be no divisions among you, but that you be united*
> *in the same mind and the same judgment."*
>
> —— **1 Corinthians 1:10** ——

In his second letter to the church, Paul focuses on calling the believers to be unified with him in ministry, as there were outsiders questioning Paul's apostleship because of the amount of suffering he'd endured.[19] As if his suffering and weakness somehow disqualified him or highlighted a lack of God's favor. However, Paul looks at his life through a gospel lens and comes to a much different conclusion.

Read 2 Corinthians 11:16–30.

● List the suffering that Paul endures.

---

19 "ESV Introductions – Study Resources." n.d. Blue Letter Bible. Accessed July 14, 2021. https://www.blueletterbible.org/study/intros/esv_intros.cfm#at_2_Corinthians.

● What is his response to his suffering?

Do you see how Paul's gospel lens sees things differently? He takes it a step further in chapter 12 by addressing his own personal weaknesses. Before we read that, take a minute to think about what you'd classify as your greatest weakness? (I won't ask you to write it down, but I do want you to hold it in your mind for just a little bit.)

● What feelings, emotions, or thoughts does that weakness bring to the surface for you?

With that in mind, read 2 Corinthians 12:1–10.

● What purpose does Paul give for the "thorn in his flesh"?

● We aren't specifically told what the "thorn" is, but it's clear that it's difficult and/or painful. What word does Paul use to describe how it affects him? (v. 7)

—Does this word resonate with your experience of weakness or suffering? Why or why not?

● Write out the Lord's response to Paul in verse 9.

● What is Paul's response?

I don't know about you, but "glad boasting" is *not* how I usually respond when face to face with my weaknesses! But don't miss the second part of verse 9—why is Paul choosing glad boasting? Fill in the blanks below:

"Therefore I will boast all the more gladly of my weaknesses so that the _____ of _____ may _____ upon me."

This changes everything! The power of God is on display when we see his grace for what it really is.

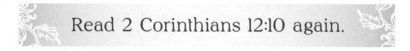

Read Romans 8:10–11.

● What power does Paul point to here?

The power of God is never clearer than in the resurrection of Jesus—the very act that bestows grace on each of us. The unmerited favor where we are given the ability to put on the righteousness of Jesus instead of being enslaved to the sin we cannot get away from!

With a view of that glorious grace, Paul is able to walk contentedly in any circumstance.

Read 2 Corinthians 12:10 again.

Content with weakness. Insult. Hardship. Persecution. Calamities. Nothing to prove because he's resting in the power of Christ and he knows that every broken way points him right to dependence on Jesus. "For when I am weak, then I am strong."

TRUTH
Weakness isn't to be feared.

GET PRACTICAL

"The gift of eternal life guarantees that I have been and will be forgiven, and that every broken thing inside me will be completely repaired."[20]

Write a prayer that begins with:

"Jesus, because of your grace, help me to gladly boast in . . ."

---

20 Paul David Tripp, *New Morning Mercies* (Wheaton, Il.: Crossway Books, 2021).

DAY 5 REFLECT

Flip through this session's personal study and write down 1–2 things that stick out to you.

1.

2.

Now, it's time to think about how this applies to your life. Here are a few prompts to get you started. Take some time to reflect and/or journal and pray over what you're learning.

- Because of grace, how are you personally "freed to do good"?

- Is your faith doing work? Are your works missing grace-fueled knowledge?

- Where are you currently feeling unworthy, ill-equipped, or insufficient? How does revisiting the truth of God's generous, unmerited favor encourage you to lean into Him?

WANTING GOD'S STORY

GROUP SESSION

OPENING

Have a volunteer read the opening out loud for the group.

The end goal of God's redeeming grace is to bring us, His children, back to Himself, as lovers and worshipers of God. This final week is about our stories, not because the goal of grace is for us to make much of our own dreams and plans, but to discover God's purposes in and through us as Christ-followers.

The stories we imagine for ourselves when we're young hold a lot of promise, don't they? They're full of degrees and careers, significant others who turn into spouses, kids, houses—they're full of hope and dreams. None of us desire stories of pain, loss, or suffering in our lives, and none of us can make sense of those pages of our stories if we don't learn to see them through the lens of grace.

What if there were a different way to think about the story of our lives? What if the grace of God not only saves us from a life of destruction but truly sustains us for a life of perseverance? What if grace reshapes the way we see our circumstances? If God's grace changes everything we believe about what we truly need (and where to find it), then grace will change how we view our stories as well . . . even now, whatever season we're in.

Focus SCRIPTURE

Open your Bibles and have a volunteer read this session's Scripture out loud for the group. It doesn't matter which translation you have—reading God's Word together is always a good idea!

1 Peter 1:6–7

Warm-Up QUESTION

Take a few moments to think about the question individually before asking for 1–2 volunteers to share their answers with the group.

Has your life followed the story line you thought it would? How has your life deviated from that same story line? What are some things you wouldn't have chosen to write into your story? Share with the group if you are willing.

WATCH THE SESSION 6 VIDEO

Feel free to use this space to take notes.

Scriptures referenced
in this session:

Romans 8:28

1 Peter 1:6, 10–12

Isaiah 61:1–3

Colossians 1:24, 26–29

Ephesians 3:21–22

Psalm 46:10

GROUP
DISCUSSION QUESTIONS

Use the following questions to help process the themes from the video session. You may not get to every question, and that's okay!

1. How have you wrestled with wanting your story more than God's story? Is there something specific that comes to mind?

2. What tensions exist for you in this "in-between" life—after salvation, but before eternal life?

3. How can you encourage each other to remember that grace is our true home?

4. What does it look like, practically, to trust God with the story He is writing for you?

5. What posture(s) do you need to adopt in order to submit to God's authorship?

PRAY

Spend some time praying together before dismissing the group.

What things do you tend to run to, other than Jesus, for self-worth, identity, or satisfaction? Jot down a few things here:

Pair up with one other woman and share your answers with each other. Take turns praying for one another, asking God to help you both believe that Jesus is better.

IN THE COMING DAYS

Make time in the coming days to work through the personal study on the following pages. Do as much as you can to get the full benefit from the teaching.

WANTING GOD'S STORY

PERSONAL STUDY

DAY 1 A TRUSTWORTHY AUTHOR

TRUTH
God writes the best stories.

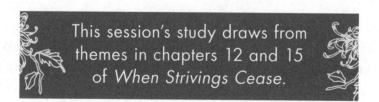

This session's study draws from themes in chapters 12 and 15 of *When Strivings Cease*.

When you think about the story of your life, where does your mind go first? To the beginning—when you were born? Or maybe to a significant turning point in your childhood? When you met your spouse? Or maybe to the twists and turns of adulthood that you could have never imagined?

The story of your life may be exactly what you thought it would be, or it may feel a little jumbled . . . but regardless of the details, you *are* part of a story that's being written by a very trustworthy author. In Psalm 139, the Bible tells us that God "knitted us together" in our mother's womb and that every day of our life was written in God's book even before we were born. Talk about an intentional God!

"For you formed my inward parts; you knitted me together in my mother's womb. I praise you, for I am fearfully and wonderfully made. Wonderful are your works; my soul knows it very well. . . . Your eyes saw my unformed substance; in your book were written, every one of them, the days that were formed for me, when as yet there was none of them."

— Psalm 139:13–14, 16 —

If you're in a particularly difficult season, or your story isn't unfolding the way you thought it would, it's tempting to doubt that God is good or trustworthy. Thankfully, the Bible tells and shows us that He is, over and over again.

Let's look at the example of Joseph in the Old Testament. He certainly couldn't have anticipated the twists and turns his life would take, but toward the end he's able to confidently proclaim the faithfulness of God.

BETRAYED

Joseph was the second-to-last son born to Jacob (also called Israel) and Rachel, and his father loved him deeply. In fact, the Bible tells us that he loved him "more than any other of his sons" (Genesis 37:3). As you might imagine, this reality caused some tension with his brothers.

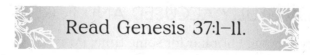

Read Genesis 37:1–11.

- What does Joseph dream about?

- Why did his brothers (and even his father) rebuke him?

At some point, while Joseph's brothers are away tending their father's flock, Jacob sends Joseph to check in with them.

Read Genesis 37:18–28.

- What did his brothers plan on doing when they saw him coming?

- What did they ultimately decide to do?

Yes, you read that right—sibling rivalry led Joseph's brothers to sell him as a slave. We don't know the exact details, but the people who bought him eventually sell him to an Egyptian man named Potiphar. And so begins the next chapter in the story of Joseph's life.

WRONGFULLY ACCUSED AND FORGOTTEN

After faithfully serving Potiphar for some time, Potiphar's wife attempts to seduce Joseph. Being a man of integrity, he refuses her advances, so she falsely accuses him of assault and Joseph is thrown into prison, where he remains for at least two years. Even in jail, Joseph gains favor with his superiors.

Read the full story of Potiphar's wife's false accusation in Genesis 39:6–20.

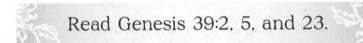

Read Genesis 39:2, 5, and 23.

- What is the recurring theme of Joseph's life, regardless of his circumstance?

SECOND IN COMMAND

Eventually, because of his (God-given) ability to interpret dreams, Joseph is called before Pharaoh. He interprets Pharaoh's dreams—foretelling seven years of plenty followed by seven years of famine—and as a reward, Pharaoh makes him second in command over all of Egypt. Forgotten in prison to ruling over Egypt in one day!

Read the full story of Joseph's introduction to Pharaoh and rise to power in Genesis 41.

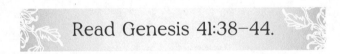

Read Genesis 41:38–44.

- Why does Pharaoh put Joseph into a position of power?

FACING THE PAST

Joseph's interpretation of Pharaoh's dreams comes true, and the famine they predicted eventually brings Joseph's brothers to Egypt in search of food. Their request brings them before Joseph—they don't realize who he is, but he recognizes them. Eventually, after Joseph is able to assess the status of his family, he reveals his identity to his brothers.

Read Genesis 45:4–15.

- How does Joseph respond to his brothers?

- How do his brothers respond to him?

- What purpose does Joseph identify in his being brought to Egypt?

GOD'S PURPOSE

Joseph's life is significant for several reasons, not the least of which is that it's how God's chosen people ended up in Egypt. His whole family comes to Egypt to live under his care, and the nation of Israel flourishes. It may seem odd, but God chose to develop his people in the midst of a foreign culture that would not accept them—so that they would be able to be set apart.

Even in his wildest dreams, I doubt that Joseph could have anticipated that God would write the story He did . . . but there was purpose in every piece of it. God planned it all, saw it all, and allowed it all to happen. He was trustworthy even when the story didn't make sense.

TRUTH
God writes the best stories.

GET PRACTICAL

Have you experienced an unexpected turn in the story of your life that you see in hindsight was in some way God's provision? Write it down as a memorial of God's faithfulness!

 **DAY 2** TREASURING CHRIST

TRUTH
Treasuring Christ is our goal.

I paraphrase Charles Spurgeon, a 19th-century English preacher, who said, "God is too good to be unkind and He is too wise to be mistaken. And when we cannot trace His hand, we must trust His heart."

It's one thing to read the quote, but as we saw with the story of Joseph yesterday, it's another thing to live it out, right? As much as we dream, scheme, and plan for a wonderful future where we achieve all our goals . . . we'd be foolish to assume that they will all happen just as we envision them.

> *"For my thoughts are not your thoughts, neither are your ways my ways, declares the Lord. For as the heavens are higher than the earth, so are my ways higher than your ways and my thoughts than your thoughts."*
>
> — **Isaiah 55:8–9** —

Where does that leave us? If the story God is writing takes us down a road we never anticipated, what do we do? What should our goal be when we're learning to trust that grace rewrites our stories both for our good and for God's glory? Just because I can acknowledge that God is a trustworthy storywriter, it doesn't mean I'm in love with the story He's writing for me.

It all boils down to where I put my confidence and what I've decided to treasure: self or Christ. It may sound harsh, but it's true. When I treasure my reputation, I will guard it and lash out at those who would threaten it. When I treasure comfort, I will complain and rebel against all that requires more than I think I ought to sacrifice. When I treasure peace at all costs, I might forfeit the truth and the hard things that must be said. When I treasure approval, I will use whatever means to gain the applause of others.

TREASURING CHRIST

So, what's the better alternative? It really is learning to treasure Christ. I know it sounds like a cliché Sunday school answer (and it is, kind of), but that doesn't make it wrong: We are made to treasure Christ above all else. And when we do, we'll find peace at every point in our story.

Let's go back to Paul's story to unpack what "treasuring Christ" means.

Read Philippians 3:1–11. Fill in the table contrasting Paul's life when his confidence is in himself with what it looks like when he's treasuring Christ.

CONFIDENCE IN HIMSELF (VV. 4–6)	TREASURING CHRIST (VV. 7–11)

Counting everything as loss feels like an overwhelming task, doesn't it? Notice the second half of verse 8, though:

". . . because of the _____ worth of knowing Christ Jesus my Lord."

The point here isn't calling everything you love trash . . . it's understanding the true value of knowing Jesus. Treasuring Christ means knowing that who He is and what He offers is better than your best-laid plans. Like the moon eclipses the sun, treasuring Christ means allowing His goodness to eclipse your hopes and dreams—to "let" Him be greater, because He is. Treasuring Christ means embracing the things He sovereignly allows in your story.

● What do you tend to treasure more than Christ?

   ☐ Reputation   ☐ Money   ☐ Approval   ☐ Ease

   ☐ Comfort   ☐ Relationships   ☐ Peace

● What would it look like for you to value Christ as an "eclipsing" good?

PRESSING ON

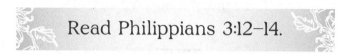

Read Philippians 3:12–14.

● What has Paul not "already obtained"? (Look back at verses 10–11).

Paul's goal is to know Christ and the power of His resurrection, to share in His suffering and to become like Him in death.

● What three actions does Paul describe in verses 13–14?

1. _____ what lies behind

2. Straining forward to what lies _____

3. _____ on toward the goal of the upward call of God in Christ Jesus

● How do each of these actions relate to treasuring Christ?

In *New Morning Mercies*, Paul David Tripp says that grace "lives at the intersection between clarity of sight and hope for the future,"[21] and it feels like

---

21 Tripp, *New Morning Mercies*, n.p.

a great summary for what Paul is saying here. Grace doesn't ignore where we've been, but it doesn't let the past define who we are, either. It gives us hope for what is possible: the upward call of God in Christ Jesus—eternal life.

When we learn to treasure Christ above all else, we wholeheartedly embrace that "God is too good to be unkind and He is too wise to be mistaken. And when we cannot trace His hand, we must trust His heart."

TRUTH
Treasuring Christ is our goal.

GET PRACTICAL

Using the actions Paul lays out in Philippians 3:13–14, think about the following questions:

- What things that "lie behind" do you need to forget in order to treasure Christ?

- What things that lie ahead will help you treasure Christ?

- How can you practically treasure Christ while pressing on toward heaven?

DAY 3 GOD'S WORKMANSHIP

TRUTH
You are God's workmanship.

Let me remind you of something amazing, friend . . . you are a work in progress.

It might not feel like an encouraging word, but I really do mean it that way! It means that when things feel intense, and the season you're in is hard, your story isn't over! Think back to Joseph's story. Until he was able to provide for his family and confront his brothers, his story didn't "make sense."

How many times do you think Joseph wondered what was happening or asked, "Why?" When he was betrayed by his brothers? Falsely accused? Imprisoned? Forgotten? Given authority over a foreign country?

I'm sure he had questions—I certainly would have! And yet, God was in control. He was intentionally forming Joseph for a future he couldn't see.

THE WORK OF HIS HANDS

It's the same for you and me. God *made* you, and He's *still making* you. He's forming you into the person He's designed you to be, and incrementally making you more like Jesus. His grace is using all the trials we think are unnecessary, all the seasons we'd rather skip, and all the seemingly insignificant tasks we can't imagine as worshipful to form us.

In Ephesians 2:10, Paul tells the believers that we are God's workmanship.

"For we are his workmanship, created in Christ Jesus for good works, which God prepared beforehand, that we should walk in them."

Ephesians 2:10

The Greek word for "workmanship" is *poiema*, which literally means "thing that is made." We get our English words for *poem* and *poetry* from it. We are the work of God's hands!

There are a handful of passages that talk about this type of workmanship—being formed, changing over time, and being made like Christ. Look up each passage and write down what you learn about being God's workmanship from it:

Isaiah 64:8	
2 Corinthians 3:16–18	
Philippians 1:6	
Romans 8:28–30	

What stands out to you from these passages? Why?

- What, if anything, from these passages frustrates you?

- What, if anything, from these passages comforts you?

Even though I'm an overachiever at heart, there's something really comforting in being reminded that not only is God not finished with me, but He has also promised to complete what He's begun in me. I will never be able to claim perfection on this side of heaven, but I know the story that God is writing is making me more like Jesus. And for that, I am so grateful.

TRUTH
You are God's workmanship.

GET PRACTICAL

When I pause long enough to take a quick survey of my own life, I can see the workmanship of God in a variety of areas:

- I'm a Chinese immigrant, who didn't speak or write English until first grade, and the Lord is using my being caught-between-two-cultures existence to teach me about citizenship in Christ.

- I'm a mom of 6 boys, and God uses my unlikeliness to show Himself as a good Father.

- I'm a late-blooming professional creative, and He used the seasons I thought were unproductive to enrich the soil that now grows visible fruit.

Where can you see God's work?

- In your trials . . .

- In what seemed unlikely . . .

- In a difficult season . . .

- In what appeared unproductive . . .

God delights to show Himself as the craftsman, the rescuer, and the author of the story of redemption—let's praise Him for it!

DAY 4 WHEN STRIVINGS CEASE

TRUTH
You can rest in Christ.

If this study accomplishes nothing else, I want you to know that in Christ, *you can stop striving*. Striving may have become your default posture, but grace—when we really understand it—says it doesn't have to be. When we learn to embrace the stories God is writing for us, treasure Christ, and revel in the fact that we're His workmanship, we can *rest*.

So much of my striving is a result of idolatry—maybe you, too? I want something more than Christ and I will do whatever it takes to make it happen. Instead of resting in the generous, unmerited favor of God, I strive and grow weary. The exhaustion of chasing after anything other than God Himself is a tiredness you feel in your bones.

When I forget the grace of God through Jesus, or don't trust that what God says is true—that it really is free—I'll look for satisfaction in a myriad of other things:

- a perfect routine
- being informed on a topic
- expressing creativity
- not letting others down
- making friends
- eating right and staying healthy
- a clean house
- disciplined children

I work to earn His favor, even though I've already been given more than I need in Christ.

INVITATIONS AND PROMISES

Fortunately, for all of us, Jesus is very clear about what it is that He—what the *gospel*—offers believers. It isn't striving, trying harder, or finishing up your to-do list. In fact, it's the opposite of all those things; it's an invitation to rest.

Read Matthew 11:25–30.

● What is the invitation in verse 28?

Note what Jesus *doesn't* say: "Come with your strategy, come with your schedules, come with your awesome track record, or come with your well-behaved children." He just invites us to come to Him.

● What are the next two invitations Jesus makes in verse 29?

Do you know what a yoke is? You've probably seen a picture of one: it's a wooden cross piece that lays over the necks of two animals and attaches to whatever it is the animals are going to pull. It basically tethers two animals to each other so they can do the job they've been assigned. When you put it that way, a yoke sounds like work, not rest, right?

So, what's Jesus getting after here? He's offering what one writer calls a "yoke exchange." "In the cross, Jesus takes our inconceivably and unbearably heavy yoke of sin's condemnation and penalty, and offers us in exchange the easy yoke and light burden of simply trusting him. He does all the work and gives us all the rest."[22]

The other instruction Jesus gives is to learn from Him. What an invitation! Jesus knows we will not know how to walk in faith, trusting in grace, unless we keep our eyes on Him. Unless we learn from His example.

- What promises does Jesus make in verses 28–30?

He promises rest twice in these verses. *True* rest when we come to Him, take His yoke, and learn from Him.

Often, when we're tired, we think we need more sleep. Maybe we're burned out, and think we need a vacation. Or, maybe we're depressed, and we think we're hopeless. In these situations, it's so tempting to turn to our idols for comfort.

- When you're weary, what idols do you tend to turn to?

The beauty of Jesus' invitation in Matthew 11 is that He will give us more than sleep, vacation, or a sliver of hope. We can find true rest in Christ's work on the cross. We can find reprieve and renewal through the promises of His Word. He offers us joy and hope in His faithfulness.

He's writing the best story, friend. He's after our hearts and His grace really can transform our lives. He has *done* the work of redemption, he *is doing* the work of sanctification, and he *will do* the work of glorification when He returns. Go to Him, and rest!

---

22 "Come, All Who Are Weary." 2016. Desiring God. May 13, 2016. https://www.desiringgod .org/articles/come-all-who-are-weary.

Redemption: God's purchase of believers made possible by the life, death, and resurrection of Jesus

Sanctification: the process of being made more like Jesus

Glorification: the ultimate perfection of believers for eternity

TRUTH
You can rest in Christ.

GET PRACTICAL

Let's look back at some of the truths we've been rehearsing in this study, all together in one place. Read the list out loud.

—The brokenness you feel is sin, and sin broke our relationship with God and His favor.

—Grace is more extravagant than we know.

—You can't earn a free gift.

—You have nothing to prove when your identity is in Christ.

—Redemption secures our belonging as beloved.

—God set the price for our welcome, and He paid it Himself.

—Grace frees when freely received.

—You've been given more than enough.

—Grace is the antidote to shame.

—Jesus bears our shame.

—There is no condemnation in Christ.

—Grace makes forgiveness possible.

—"Better" is a never-ending trap that can't save you.

—Grace completely transforms us.

—You are a new creation.

—Grace allows us to experience true peace.

—Because Jesus is worthy, we become worthy by grace.

—Good works are only as fruitful as we are deeply rooted in grace.

—True faith works.

—Weakness isn't to be feared.

—God writes the best stories.

—Treasuring Christ is the goal.

—You are God's workmanship.

—You can rest in Christ.

- Which one is the easiest for you to believe, grasp, and/or practice? Why?

- How can you continue to rehearse this truth in your life regularly?

- Which one is the most difficult for you to believe, grasp, and/or practice? Why?

- How can you begin to rehearse this truth in your life regularly?

DAY 5 REFLECT

Flip through this session's personal study and write down 1–2 things that stick out to you.

1.

2.

3. Now, it's time to think about how this applies to your life. Here are a few prompts to get you started. Take some time to reflect and/or journal and pray over what you're learning.

● What are the parts of your story that feel the hardest to accept? How can you embrace them because of grace?

● What does it look like to practically treasure Christ? Who might be able to walk alongside you in practicing it?

● How has your view of grace changed over the course of this study? What new insights do you have? How will they affect your life?

CONCLUSION

I shared my heart in the teaching video accompanying this session and wanted to repeat it here: If I have one fear as we come to our final time together, it's that you could walk away from these weeks of study and somehow return to the persuasive lullaby the world sings over you. It's the one that continually repeats,

"It's all about you."
"How do you feel about God's Word?"
"Go get what you deserve."
"Does believing in God actually make my life better?"
"Try harder—you're almost perfect."
"How can God make my dreams come true?"

I know the enemy will try to convince you that God's grace is the story of your effort, instead of His favor. I know it because for so many years of my life, it's how I operated. I wish someone had looked past the good-daughter, good-friend, good-student, good-Christian facade of my youth and called me out on my Jesus-plus-my-own-efforts kind of living!

So, I hope that's exactly what this study has done for you. The invitation is clear, friend—you can lay your burdens down! In Christ, you have been given the generous, unmerited favor of God, and there's *nothing* you can do to make yourself more loved or more favored than you already are. Let's rest in Him and find no greater call to cease striving, nor greater fuel to start freely living, than the wondrous, life-transforming grace of our good God.

Because of *amazing* grace,

— Ruth

LEADER'S GUIDE

GROUP SIZE

The *When Striving's Cease* video curriculum is designed to be experienced in a group setting such as a Bible study, small group, or during a weekend retreat. After watching each video session, you and the members of your group will participate in a time of discussion and reflection on what you've learned. If you have a larger group (more than 12 people), consider breaking up into smaller groups during the discussion time.

MATERIALS NEEDED

Each participant should have their own study guide, which includes space to take video notes, group discussion questions, and a personal study section to deepen learning between sessions.

FACILITATION

Each group should appoint a facilitator who is responsible for starting the video and keeping track of time during the activities and discussion. Facilitators may also read questions aloud, monitor discussions, prompt participants to respond, and ensure everyone has the opportunity to participate.

APPENDIX
AN INVITATION[23]

Dear friend,

If you're jumping into this study and feel like an outsider when it comes to understanding God's faithfulness in salvation, welcome. This study is for you, too! Maybe your faith journey hasn't felt much like the grace of God you're reading about here or in God's Word. Or, maybe you've tasted and seen the grace of God and today is your new beginning to walk in that grace.

The gospel—the good news of Jesus Christ—is simply this:

The end of earning His favor *A beginning in forgiveness*
The end of slavery to sin *A beginning in freedom*
The end of being "good enough" *A beginning in surrender*
The end of self-reliance *A beginning in holiness*
The end of condemnation *A beginning in loving Christ more*

A love story told from the beginning of time starts in the garden, where Adam and Eve knew no separation from their Creator until they exchanged transparency with their God for sinful pride. It's the story of how that same God orchestrated and wooed His people for generations so that they might know the weight of their sin and their need for a Savior. That Savior was Jesus, who lived a sinless life for 33 years on earth in order to fulfill the will of the Father by dying a criminal's death on the cross to pay the penalty of man's disobedience—the penalty of separation that you and I would suffer if not for His shed blood. And so, the invitation and welcome is yours: to come as broken, hopeless, and burdened . . . and find peace for your soul.

Because of grace,

— Ruth

---

23 Adapted from *GraceLaced*, Ruth Chou Simons (Eugene, Ore.: Harvest House Publishers, 2017).

Grace Secures What Striving Cannot

In this hustling, image-forward age of opportunity and affirming social media memes, we feel more anxious than ever. And we end up constantly feeling like we're behind, lacking, and failing—at home, at work, with friends, with God.

With personal stories, biblical wisdom, and original artwork by Ruth, *When Strivings Cease* guides you on a journey to find true freedom from the never-ending quest for self-improvement—because in Christ you are enough.

9781400224999

Available now wherever books are sold.

NELSON BOOKS

An Imprint of Thomas Nelson